siblings

Related title from David Fulton Publishers:

Moving On: Supporting Parents of Children with SEN
Alison Orphan
1-84312-113-1

siblings

Coming unstuck and putting back the pieces

Kate Strohm

David Fulton Publishers

David Fulton Publishers Ltd
The Chiswick Centre, 414 Chiswick High Road, London W4 5TF

www.fultonpublishers.co.uk

This edition published by arrangement with Wakefield Press, Australia
First published in Great Britain in 2004 by David Fulton Publishers

David Fulton Publishers is a division of Granada Learning, part of ITV plc.

10 9 8 7 6 5 4 3 2 1

British Library Cataloguing in Publication Data
A catalogue record for this book is available from the British Library.

ISBN 1 84312 232 4

Typeset by Clinton Ellicott, Wakefield Press
Printed and bound in Great Britain

For Helen – next time, together, you and I
will sing and dance with the fairies.

Give sorrow words; the grief that does not speak knits up the overwrought heart and bids it break.

–William Shakespeare, *Macbeth*

Contents

Foreword

The birth of a child with a disability or the onset of a chronic life-threatening illness in a young child is a devastating event for most parents – it shatters many of their hopes and expectations. It poignantly reminds us that, despite all that medical science and we can do, life isn't fair – more so for some than others.

While our concerns focus naturally on the affected child and their parents, less attention is given to other siblings. We worry about the child with the disability – the pain of repeated medical interventions, and the impact of the disability on all aspects of their development. We also worry about how the parents are coping emotionally, the impact on their relationship with each other and their child, and the implications for their finances and careers. Siblings, on the other hand, are often the forgotten ones.

The plight of siblings was brought home to me as I spoke to people after reading Kate Strohm's manuscript. I met grown-up siblings who remembered feelings of ambivalence very similar to those Kate has described; also siblings who remembered feeling they were never the centre of their parents' attention, because of the overwhelming demands on their parents of caring for their brother or sister. And I spoke to people who knew siblings in the midst of troubled adult lives, and wondered about the impacts of their experiences, given that their early lives had seemed so full of promise.

Siblings is a book that should be read by anyone coming into contact with a family that includes a child with a disability, whether through their work or socially. Those who assist families who have a child with a disability will find it full of rich insights that can help them in their work – with parents, with the young person with the disability and now, just as importantly, with that child's siblings.

This is also a valuable book for parents who face the challenge of having a child with a disability in their family. But it is especially valuable to siblings themselves. As they get older, the brothers and sisters of young people with a disability will see many aspects of their own experience mirrored in the words of others who have shared their insights with Kate. They will find that they no longer need to be in the shadow and are no longer alone. And for them, the sense of connection that flows from that may bring them a sense of peace that they have not experienced before.

Kate Strohm has done all of us a wonderful service in providing a perspective that has until now been largely overlooked.

Graham Vimpani, MBBS, PhD, FRACP, FAFPHM
Professor of Paediatrics and Child Health
University of Newcastle
Australia

Preface

As a child I had a recurrent dream in which I was sitting on a concrete slab in the middle of a rough ocean. The slab reached down to the ocean floor, like a huge pylon, but was very small in area. I didn't have much room to move.

Many years later the dream revisited me and this time its message was clearer. I had been closely exploring my experience of being a sibling of someone with a disability, and starting to unravel a whole range of mixed feelings. Although it had been more than 30 years since the dream was a regular feature of my night-time imaginings, it felt instantly familiar. It seemed to say that although I had a true sense of belonging as a child, with deep connections to a loving family, I also felt alone and afraid.

Feelings of isolation and fear had been a part of my life for as long as I could remember, even though they were not apparent to people around me. Outwardly, I appeared confident and successful. In fact, in my thirties I was becoming a household name on South Australian radio station SA.FM and its network around Australia. At the same time, another side of me struggled with fear and panic, and a large part of my life was spent escaping what were for me difficult situations, socially and at work.

Another ten years passed before I started to understand this other side of me. Through talking with other siblings, reading and seeking help through therapy, I started to uncover the secrets I had been hiding, especially from myself. I discovered a vast amount of literature on the concerns of children who grow up with a brother or sister with special needs. I talked to a host of siblings and found out I was not alone. Others were experiencing similar feelings and confusion. These discussions were the impetus for writing this book.

During a trip to the United States in 1998 I had contact with a number of siblings and people involved with sibling programs. I decided to set up a program in Australia. Siblings Australia Inc. has become a thriving national program. It provides direct services to families, both parents and siblings, and also works closely with service providers to improve the support given to families.

Who should read this book?

The purpose of this book is to raise awareness of sibling issues, give siblings a voice, and outline a range of strategies to help siblings become stronger. The information contained here is based essentially on the personal reflections of families and, in particular, siblings, together with extensive research of international material on sibling issues.

As a sibling you will read this book and discover that you are not alone in your experiences and feelings; that growing up with a brother or sister with special needs has shaped who you are and how you operate in the world.

Through their relationships with their brothers and sisters, children learn to express emotions and feelings such as love, loyalty, anger and rivalry. They gain companionship and support and learn to give and take. Siblings help teach each other social skills and play a part in each other's identity development. When one sibling has special needs, some aspects of the relationship can change enormously.

Until now most of the stories we have heard from siblings reflect a positive experience because they are the easy stories to tell. It seems they are the only stories that society wants to hear. But as you will read here, that is not the reality for many. Not everyone gains inspiration or feels especially blessed by having a brother or sister with special needs. It is often difficult to be honest when our culture tells us constantly that we must be 'plucky' or 'perky'. The most helpful thing in my own journey of acceptance was hearing others express mixed feelings that were similar to my own.

As a parent reading this book you will understand more fully the concerns of your able children and how you can support them. Through that awareness you will feel more competent as a parent and will be able to help your whole family to be stronger and more supportive of each other.

Many of the examples I cite focus on the difficulties siblings face. Many of the experiences reflect some criticism of the way parents handle certain situations. I don't include these to add to any self-doubt or guilt you may feel as a parent. Most siblings recognise the burden their parents carry. Parents rarely receive the support they need in the early stages of adjustment. To explore and learn from these situations, however, it is necessary to look at these stories.

At times you may feel like 'piggy in the middle', trying to meet the needs of all the members of your family while still struggling with your own mixed feelings of grief and acceptance. I do not wish to alarm you. Children can be resilient and often need very little in order to adjust positively. If you understand that siblings within your family are facing particular difficulties, both you and all your children can benefit. With support, parents are usually able to regain a sense of control over their lives, hope for the future and renewed self-confidence. At the same time, you can help your children adjust and grow from their experience.

As a practitioner working with families that include a child with special needs, this book will help you more fully understand the concerns of siblings and how they can best be supported.

It took me more than 30 years to find a professional who could help me make some sense of my own confused feelings. Things have come a long way in terms of disability acceptance and understanding the effects on families, but there is still a way to go. Through my work with Siblings Australia, I see young children who struggle with their family situation and who have had no support to deal with their difficulties. I have contact with practitioners who have little understanding of sibling issues.

The problem is not the person with special needs; it is the level of support given to families of such children. A growing advocacy movement and a trend toward early intervention for children who have special needs are both welcome signs of improved community awareness. At the same time, there need to be help and support for both siblings and parents. In order to build strong, united families, we must enable parents themselves to develop strength. With support, siblings will emerge from the shadows of self-doubt, of fear, embarrassment, anger and guilt. They can then assume their own important place in their family, and in society.

What is meant by 'special needs'

Throughout the book I focus on intellectual and physical disabilities. Through talking with families and health practitioners, and reading widely, it has become clear that the needs of siblings can be looked at in a much broader context. Mental illness, chronic illness, genetic disorders, cardiac problems, cancer and HIV-related illness, premature babies and a range of other situations that create special needs all leave siblings dealing with a number of stresses. This stress is often quite difficult to deal with at a young age, when understanding and emotional maturity are still developing.

I write essentially about special needs that are present from birth, even though diagnosis may take some time. Of course, many special needs arise later. A child may have an acquired brain injury due to an accident or cerebral haemorrhage, or develop a chronic illness at an older age. Mental illness can manifest at various stages in a person's life and interfere with family relationships.

In all of these situations the family system undergoes a shift, each family member is affected, and siblings need similar types of support.

Siblings in Australia

There are hundreds of thousands of siblings of people with special needs in Australia. According to the Australian Institute of Health and Welfare (from estimates made of the Australian Bureau of Statistics, 1998 *Survey of Disability, Ageing and Carers* confidentialised unit record file), there are up to 200,000 people under the age of 25 with a severe or profound disability or chronic illness. We can assume that each of these people, on average, would have at least one sibling. (There are around 296,000 children in the UK with SEN.)

SANE Australia, a national charity that helps people affected by mental illness, states in its literature that 'in Australia alone there are over 200,000 people who are siblings of people seriously affected by mental illness'.

The use of language

Throughout the book I alternate between using the words *disability* and *special needs. Special needs* is a broader term that covers a wider range of situations. However, at times I use the word *disability* if it seems appropriate.

Throughout the book, when referring to *siblings*, I mean brothers and sisters of people with special needs. I sometimes use the term *single sibling* when referring to children who have no other brothers or sisters apart from the child with special needs. I sometimes use the term *able sibling* when referring to a child without special needs. I also alternate between the use of *he* and *she* when referring to individual siblings.

A number of terms are used to refer to the people who work with families. The term *service provider* refers to a range of organisations and individuals with which a family comes into contact if they have a child with special needs. Organisations might include hospitals, disability services and schools. Individuals include doctors, nurses, physiotherapists, speech pathologists, psychologists and social workers. Other terms that might be used include *health professional* and *practitioner.*

In recent times there has been a growing trend to use people-first language. Instead of labelling someone as 'retarded' or 'crippled', the preference is to refer to a 'person with an intellectual or physical disability'. This allows a person to be seen more easily in ways other than in terms of his disability only. However, when quoting others I use their words, which do not necessarily reflect my own preferences.

Throughout the book, the majority of quotes are from women: mothers or sisters of people with disabilities. I do not wish to imply that fathers and brothers are immune from the concerns expressed here; in fact the opposite is true. It happened that most of the parents who came to various focus groups were mothers; most of the siblings I managed to interview were sisters; and the majority of contributors to the internet sibling discussion group I participate in are women.

When referring to families, I sometimes use the word *marriage*, but acknowledge that there are other living arrangements that are equally as committed. I also understand that many parents don't have a partner and are sole parents.

When referring to the effects of a child's disability on a family, I concentrate on parents and siblings. Grandparents, other extended family members and close friends can also be affected by the disability. In turn, their reactions can affect the beliefs and attitudes of the family, and they can be an important source of support.

Learning from one another

Finally, having acknowledged that much of this book focuses on the difficulties of having a child with special needs in the family, it is true that many families are able to manage the challenges and become enriched by their experiences. I am moved by the courage and inspiration some families display. Siblings, in particular, can develop a range of positive qualities and many feel they have benefited enormously from their particular family circumstances. If children experience major stresses in childhood and learn ways of coping positively, they can in fact be strengthened by those difficulties. With support, siblings are not only able to reach their own potential but also contribute to the quality of life of their brother or sister with special needs. We need to learn from all families, from both their positive and negative experiences. I do not pretend to have all the answers, but I hope the ideas in this book will help build links between siblings, between parents and siblings, and, finally, between practitioners and families.

Kate Strohm, Adelaide, 2002

My Story

1

A shared childhood

After marrying in Adelaide in 1947, my parents set up house in Thevenard, a small coastal town on the far west coast of South Australia. It was a happy time for them, with numerous friends and family nearby. A year later their happiness seemed complete with the news that they were expecting their first child.

There were concerns for some months before the birth because the baby was in the wrong position, but just before my mother went into labour the baby turned. Labour itself was a lonely, frightening experience for Mum. In those days, the father was virtually dismissed at the doorway; my mother was left alone in the small country hospital for hours at a time. Eventually a baby girl, Helen, was born.

Within days, my parents suspected that something was amiss. My sister could not keep milk down. She vomited constantly. The local doctor kept dismissing my parents' fears, insisting my sister 'merely' had congenital stenosis of the oesophagus (a narrowing of the oesophagus, which itself can be quite serious). Mum would put her baby in the sun to kick. In time, it became obvious that she could kick with only one leg. Slowly, joy turned to apprehension. At nine months of age my sister was flown to Adelaide for medical tests and my parents' worst fears were realised. They were told she had cerebral palsy.

In order to access specialised care for their new baby, my parents moved to Adelaide. Soon after the move, my mother took my sister to a local doctor. He said my parents should place her in an institution and forget about her. Mum insisted that she wanted to care for her baby – the baby showed so much affection – to which the doctor replied, 'So does a cat or dog if you are kind to it.' My parents never went to that doctor again.

Helen had suffered a cerebral haemorrhage, either before or during birth, which had affected one side of her brain. She was partially paralysed on one side of her body. As a child she wore 'leg irons' and a brace for her right hand. She walked with an unsteady gait. She could not shower or dress herself. Her throat muscles were affected, which meant she could not speak or swallow properly. She dribbled; Mum would mash her food first and then Helen would eat by pushing one mouthful down with the next. She could make some sounds but none that were easily intelligible. The extent of her intellectual disabilities was unknown and is still difficult to assess.

After much apprehension, my parents decided to have another child. When I was born in 1953, my sister was nearly four years old. My early childhood memories are not clear. Some things I have been told, others I vaguely recollect. I have a sense of being surrounded by love, but I also remember the ongoing stress within our family.

When I was a baby and needed to sleep, my mother barricaded me in my room for safety. It was difficult for my sister to understand that this new baby was not a toy, and she would be quite rough and hurt me. Jealousy probably played a part in this as well.

Her delayed development meant that she learnt to walk just before I did. Often, just as I would get upright, she would push me over. She was strong, in spite of her disabilities. As we grew older, we would sometimes fight, and I would often be the one hurt. I am told there were other times when we interacted quite happily.

When my sister was about four she went to Ashford House, a school in Adelaide for children with disabilities. She would be taken to school in a bus. As I grew older, I thought the bus was extremely special and delighted in greeting it each morning. I'd hop into my sister's seat until it was time for the bus to go. Helen was fearful of everything, especially leaving home, and would struggle with my mother against being put on the bus, even though she enjoyed her time at school.

Although my sister could not talk, she understood much of what went on around her. She would 'talk' about things –

Christmas, birthdays, other happenings – with actions and sounds. It was often like the 'I've got a secret' guessing game. My uncle wanted to teach her signing, but the speech pathologists of the day forbade it, saying that she needed to keep working her throat muscles. In fact, they never improved and her inability to communicate effectively has been a major frustration for both her and the rest of our family.

Part of my sister's condition includes epilepsy, which is now largely controlled by medication. But as a child she would have regular turns, known as petit mal seizures, which caused her to stare, and her facial muscles to twist. These would last for several seconds and be followed by prolonged crying. I never really understood what was happening, but remember as a young child being frightened by these incidents. I don't recall my parents explaining them in terms that I understood. There was no opportunity to discuss my feelings.

My mother regularly invited children to our house to play. If new children seemed worried by Helen's strange behaviour, Mum would take them aside to explain that even though my sister couldn't talk and play, she could understand what was being said, and enjoyed being a part of our activities. I think, at that age and in that situation, I was quite comfortable with her being with us all. The children seemed to accept her differences.

It was a different matter when we were out. It upset me when people stared, both for my own sake and for Helen, who I wanted to protect. People would actually stop in their tracks and watch our slow progress. This annoyed my parents as well, not only because they could see that I was distressed, but because they were unable to provide an appropriate answer to my question of why people stared. To this day people still stare and we still feel uncomfortable.

As a child I did well at school. I played netball, took part in callisthenics and had several friends. At home I tried to be 'good', to achieve and to 'make things right' for my parents. But inside there was a growing collection of feelings that confused me and which I could not share with anyone. I felt so sorry for my sister but, because of the embarrassment she unintentionally caused me, I wished she would disappear. I felt bad whenever I achieved some feat that my sister could not. At the same time, I was constantly seeking approval.

For many years my sister cried at night. She and I shared a room. My father needed to go to work each day and I needed to go to school. In order for us to get some sleep, Mum would shift to sleep in my bed and I would sleep with Dad. It was exhausting for everyone. Eventually, in my early teens, my parents built on an extra room for me, which meant that I could have some privacy and a quiet space for study.

My sister would sometimes stay at Somerton Home, an Adelaide facility that provided respite for families, but I remember her desperately not wanting to go. With all the distress surrounding her departures, and because we were all left feeling full of sorrow and guilt, it was difficult to enjoy our break.

Our lives revolved around my sister's needs. We didn't do a lot of the things other families did. One year we went to the Royal Adelaide Show. My sister saw an ambulance and wouldn't come out of the chicken pavilion because she associated ambulances with being taken away from home. We didn't go to the Show again.

The few times I went out to dinner alone with my parents were precious. Occasionally I took part in an activity with one parent but it was a rare moment, indeed, when I had both parents' sole attention. At those times I felt like a princess.

Fortunately, we were able to holiday with my mother's relatives in the country. A supportive extended family had many benefits for me. Spending time with cousins helped the development of my social skills. At times I would visit them on my own, which increased my ability to develop independence. Two of my grandparents provided tremendous support when I was young. My paternal grandmother often cared for us and I'll always remember her ability to jolly Helen along.

Helen attended Ashford House for 26 years. It was a wonderful facility that celebrated the lives of all its students. During that time Helen continued to have physiotherapy and speech therapy. Her formal schooling was limited. In later years she was transferred to the Activity Centre, where she learnt to help with the cooking and crafts. She also joined the Brownie troupe at the school. As a family we attended many fetes, barbecues and concerts, cricket days and other celebrations.

At the age of 30 my sister moved from Ashford House to a sheltered workshop. She would often become highly emotional and refuse to go. Staying home was not the best option for her and, acting on professional advice, my parents placed her in residential care during the week. This was a particularly difficult transition for everyone.

After some time, Helen settled into supported accommodation and a sheltered workshop. She has been a valued employee for many years and, although sometimes tentative, continues to find enjoyment in a range of activities. She spends weekends and holidays with my parents, follows football and loves music and discos. My parents have continued to give her tremendous care and loyalty for more than 50 years. She gains enormous pleasure from being around friends and family. At social gatherings she takes particular pride in showing off her family, especially my husband, our two children and myself. And though it is difficult for her to initiate conversations herself, she responds to many situations with a great deal of interest and humour.

2

Coming unstuck and putting back the pieces

As a child I had a solid foundation, with nurturing parents and a warm extended family. At one level my self-worth was strong. At another level, however, the stresses undermined that foundation and my self-esteem. I was incapable of understanding, let alone expressing, the effect of growing up with my sister.

In my early teens it all caught up with me. I started to develop insomnia and my parents could see that suddenly I had lost all confidence. At school, even the simplest task of calling out and spelling my name would send me into a spin. I thought that my voice shook and I would panic, afraid of what others would think. I thought if I showed any lack of control that people might think there was something wrong with me. I was convinced I was ugly. I was a prefect at my high school for several years and one year I was also elected house captain. It would seem that I was popular and able to carry out many normal activities, but inside I was full of self-doubt. I became an expert at hiding the panic that was eating away at me.

My parents took me at different times to a psychologist, a hypnotherapist and a psychiatrist. They all said there was nothing wrong with me. One of the doctors put me on Valium to help me sleep. He also tried desensitising therapy, where I had to read in front of a group of people in which the numbers gradually increased, but this had no effect. No one thought to explore my family situation.

As my fears grew, I kept pushing myself to achieve and to try to overcome them. The more I tried, the worse my fears became.

During high school I wanted to be a doctor or teacher. Too nervous to attempt either because of my anxiety of being watched, I chose Applied Science, thinking that laboratory work would be less threatening. Once I reached university, tutorials were hell. At times I walked the corridors, having escaped in a panic from a room full of people.

The anger I felt toward myself was enormous. Later, in various work situations, having a tea break with others became a nightmare. During the time I was involved in discussions, I felt afraid that someone would ask me a question; the focus would then be on me – I might appear nervous and would be judged badly as a result. I was always more nervous when eating was involved. In many ways I felt like I had a split personality. Others saw me as having plenty of confidence. I was gregarious, fun-loving and joined in social activities, but I always felt anxious. If my hands or voice shook, or if I blushed, it seemed like the end of the world.

In my twenties, having graduated from university and worked in various hospitals, I travelled overseas frequently. I realise now that in some ways these trips were escapes from my tension and anxiety. They were fun and carefree times. But when I came back to my life in Australia, the old bogies would return. In spite of my fears, I kept pushing myself to be involved in activities that made me uncomfortable.

I pursued more study, and during that period started working at the Institute for Fitness Research and Training (IFRT) in Adelaide. While there I desperately wanted to teach fitness classes. Though I was very nervous, I was able to manage both the training and the teaching. Looking back on that time, I realise that I was able to teach in that setting because I could keep moving. Even though I was the teacher, the focus was not solely on me and, when it was, we would all be exercising. This alleviated any feeling of being trapped and, as I became comfortable with the setting, I even enjoyed the performance.

During my time at the IFRT I was offered the chance to produce and present a daily health segment, 'Body Language', on radio station SA.FM. Though incredibly nervous in the beginning, I managed because I taped the show in front of a single sound technician. My segment would be listened to by hundreds of thousands of people, but I couldn't see them and, more importantly, they couldn't see me. 'Body Language' became an integral part of the Austereo network's programming for several years. I loved the recognition radio work gave me, but at another level I felt a fraud. Radio station parties – where I could mingle freely with no chance of being the focus of attention – were fine, but more formal dinners were torture for me. The panic would rise.

Eventually I was appointed a health educator in a community health centre – my dream job. I had studied and worked for years to attain this position and there was so much I loved about it – but in the end my fear got the better of me. I lived in dread of the weekly staff meeting, where someone might ask me a question. I felt completely capable in my role and knew I was doing the job well, but the idea of speaking in the group filled me with panic. I feared I would be seen as unprofessional if I appeared nervous or awkward. I always sat near the door so I had an easy escape should the need arise. Often, when the anxiety became too much, I pretended to have a coughing fit, but there was a limit to how many times I could use that as an escape. I used up so much energy in trying to hide my panic that I became exhausted. The stress became too much and so I quit. I never considered talking to any of my fellow workers about my fears, but instead used the demands of my radio work as my excuse. Everyone thought I was a success, but I felt a failure.

I would experience panic attacks in other settings, too. Whenever I was suddenly the centre of attention, I would feel trapped, especially if eating at a table, and want to disappear through the floor.

I felt that somehow my fears were connected with having grown up with an older sister born with cerebral palsy. Over the years I sought various types of therapy in an attempt to deal with the panic attacks, but my feelings about my sister were never explored. Most of the therapists used a 'behavioural approach', which tried to help me find other ways of dealing with the panic when it surfaced. None of these approaches worked. It always came down to me having to change, and I never could, which made me feel even more of a failure.

Around this time I met my husband-to-be, Rob. After several months, when our relationship started to become more serious, I realised that I would need to tell him about my secret. I had been to a wedding with him where I had sat in panic for most of the time. No one else would have noticed. I told him that I had something important to tell him and asked if we could go for a walk. It seems strange now, but at the time I needed to summon all my courage.

Inwardly, as he told me later, Rob was concerned that an old boyfriend had returned to the scene or that I had some life-threatening disease. His reaction to my news was one of relief, but he didn't really understand the significance of what I had disclosed. Over the years he would come to understand more clearly.

I kept pushing myself, wearing myself out trying to hide my fears. Over and again, I sought out a new therapist, but would end up feeling worse. And still, no one really explored my childhood experiences.

During my mid-thirties, I gave birth to two daughters and most of my energies were directed to them, although I continued to work part-time on radio and as a freelance health educator. I was still troubled by my reactions in certain situations. When my elder daughter started kindergarten, I would have liked to be on committees, but fear stopped me. Even an introductory session at my daughter's school, where we had to introduce ourselves to a group of other parents, was a threat. Going out to lunch with a group of mothers could leave me feeling incredibly angry with myself and wrung out from hiding my anxiety.

When I was in my forties, I finally found a therapist who helped me sort through my confused feelings toward both myself and my sister. Part of the process involved group therapy sessions held very early in the morning. I avoided telling others what I was doing; when we had friends stay with us, I would make up a story to cover my departure for group therapy. I felt uncomfortable with the deception, but was still unable to disclose what I was doing. I began to realise that here was the crux of my problem. Deep down I was full of self-doubt. I had spent my whole life trying to hide my 'problem' from others, at enormous expense to my wellbeing.

Therapy was able to help me along the long path towards self-acceptance, although the process was exhausting and difficult. There were so many barriers. I talked and intellectualised a lot. I felt anything that drew attention to me was bad. I was afraid I was taking too much of the therapist's attention and being self-indulgent. I feared he would grow impatient and tire of me. I was still acting like a child, wanting his permission and approval, and fearing rejection.

Part of my difficulty with therapy had been my inability to acknowledge that it was acceptable to be looking at my difficulties and anxiety. When this particular therapist told me that yes, it was important to be looking at these issues and that I was okay, he gave me the permission I had been seeking. His response brought a flood of tears. Instead of trying to change my behaviour through therapies, I realised it was important to work on acceptance and understanding.

I began to understand that from an early age I had feared that if I showed any loss of control – for example, if my hands shook or my voice trembled – people might think I was like my sister, that there was something wrong with me too. I needed to be perfect and came to be terrified of others' judgements of me. As a small child I had made a decision 'not to make waves'. I wanted to make life easy for my parents, to make up for their pain. In many ways, I myself took on a parental role, wanting to protect and look after them. I couldn't bear the idea of disappointing them; I needed their approval. At some level, I knew all their expectations of raising a grown, healthy woman rested on me.

I needed to be perfect, but on another level I felt guilty about all the things I could do and achieve, but my sister could not.

I felt a range of negative feelings toward my sister, but also incredible sorrow for the life she led. I resented all the attention she received and wished I could have more. When I did get attention I felt guilty and unworthy. None of my concerns ever seemed as important as hers. I experienced guilt about most of my feelings and couldn't express any of them; they seemed to be pushed to an innermost corner, out of reach to me and to others. If these feelings escaped, I thought, people might see me for who I really was: someone who wanted my own sister to disappear. I was full of shame.

Through a year of group therapy I came to understand my reactions even more. I needed to look at a range of issues, including the belief system that had guided me. It was clear that at some point the development of my identity had been hindered and I had particular difficulty with negative emotions. The group was important in that it drew from the members some of the emotions that were suppressed within our own families. It highlighted many of my reactions and helped my understanding.

As I started to unravel my confusion, I began writing about my experiences. It was partly cathartic, a way of getting it all out of my system, and partly to help parents and therapists understand the concerns of siblings.

Slowly I opened up to close friends about what I was doing. My husband and I had numerous discussions about my reluctance to tell others about my fears and my therapy. I worried that he and others would think I was just looking for attention. I still needed permission to be more open.

During this time I joined a public-speaking group. The members were very supportive, and I was able to practise what I feared most. Many people have problems with public speaking; I probably would have been anxious with this activity even if I hadn't grown up in my family. There were, however, other levels to the anxiety that were deep and terrifying. They were connected in some way to shame and a fear that people would discover the *real* me. They revolved around my identity – who I was and who I was to become.

I wonder when I fully realised that I would not become like my sister. This has nothing to do with rational thinking. I knew I was intelligent and capable, but inside a little child still cried out for reassurance.

In my professional life I still struggled with fear and panic in certain settings. During 1997, after leaving the radio network, I took a position that involved attending meetings. I hoped I could manage, but it was only a matter of weeks before I went home in tears. I sat near the door during my first staff meeting so that I had an easy escape, but still felt an overwhelming anxiety that made me feel physically sick. I feared I would be judged as inadequate and unprofessional if I showed any signs of being nervous when speaking. I remember on one occasion fleeing the office in a panic.

I felt I had no choice but to quit. Instead, through talking with my husband, I realised that I needed to talk about the problem with someone at work. For the first time in my professional life I explained my concerns to a fellow worker, who reassured me that she would help and I could still do the job. The relief was enormous. Having someone who knew about my fears and who could cover for me, if needed, helped me to continue.

About this time, and while still taking part in group therapy, I regularly encountered two sisters at my daughter's school, which had quite an extensive program for children with disabilities. One of the sisters, who used a wheelchair, had cerebral palsy. When I first saw these two children my heart went out to the 'other' child. I wanted to rush up to staff and say, 'Make sure you look after this little one, she needs your attention too.' I didn't – that would have been inappropriate – but I started to wonder how I could help people understand more about the difficulties of siblings of children with disabilities.

That was the beginning of the process that led to this book. It took me a long time to build up the courage to write it. Although I received encouragement when talking to professionals who worked in the disability field, often my inner censor took over and the idea of writing about my experiences would be put aside. In some ways, I needed permission.

As a way to cope with this, I decided to interview other siblings of people with special needs and include their experiences in my writing. My opening-up gave them permission to be more open too. There were often tears as we shared our stories, but we all benefited from the telling. During a trip to the United States with my husband and children in 1998, I made contact with more siblings and kept hearing stories similar to my own. I met a researcher, a sibling himself, who had spent years looking at sibling issues. I was surprised to find that this was an established area of research. I spent hours poring over the books in his office, as well as books from the public library. I joined a discussion group on the internet with siblings around the world and began to see that siblings everywhere had similar reactions to mine. Some talked of being high achievers – the 'good' girl or boy in their family – but at the same time told how they struggled with different degrees of depression, anxiety, guilt and grief. It was an incredible journey of validation for me.

Back in Adelaide I set up Siblings Australia to support siblings of children with special needs and to raise awareness of their concerns. The Project is based in the Department of Psychological Medicine of the Women's and Children's Hospital in Adelaide – for full contact details, see the resources list at the back of this book.

The pressure I continue to place on myself to be perfect, to not let others down, still controls aspects of my life, but I am finding greater self-acceptance. I still grapple with my feelings toward my sister. If I don't have contact with her I feel guilty and if I do, I still feel guilty. I am embarrassed and anxious around her. I wish I could find the inspiration and devotion of which others talk. I feel such grief when I think of her life. I feel uncomfortable in the place where she lives and wonder if she does too. I wonder if she compares her life to mine. Often, after spending time with her, it takes some hours for a vague melancholy to lift. I wish I had a closer relationship with Helen, but at the same time I am noticing a gradual change in my attitude toward her, a growing acceptance of who she is. I also feel that I'm coming to terms with the confusion of feelings I experience about her. I understand and accept the need to play a greater part in her life when my parents are no longer here.

My research and travel have taught me that my story is not unique. I wish I had made contact with other siblings at a young age – what a difference that would have made to how I viewed myself. I am reminded of a story about two young boys who were friends at school. They each had a brother with disabilities but did not disclose the fact to the other. Feeling shame, they never invited the other to their home. It was only years later that they made the discovery and realised what, through fear, they had missed.

Other sibling stories

3

A lone journey

I felt completely isolated. I thought I couldn't share any of that part of my life with my friends. They didn't understand and I felt alienated from them. Other kids never had the same responsibility. – *Meagan*

Isolation is a common experience among siblings. Many lack the opportunity to talk about their feelings and their home environment and sense from their parents that these are difficult subjects. As young children their understanding of the situation is limited and this can lead to fear and anxiety. As they move through their school years they may sense how their lives are different to those of their peers. Society sends them the message that others in the same situation have a largely positive experience and those who don't are selfish. It can be extremely difficult for siblings to ask for support. They don't want to be seen as complaining and feel that they should be able to handle their situation.

Some time ago I was being interviewed on a local radio station about Siblings Australia. Nance, aged 28, whose younger brother has intellectual disabilities, phoned in to talk about her own reactions.

I can't begin to describe my relief when I first heard about a support group for brothers and sisters of people with disabilities. For all these years it was something I so desperately wanted but feared to articulate in case people thought I could not handle the responsibility or was somehow not grateful for being normal.

Siblings don't always know how to respond to others' reactions, such as awkwardness and teasing, and feel alone with the conflicting loyalties they experience. This leads many siblings to keep their feelings to themselves.

It was not until I reached my mid-forties that I shared my experiences with another sibling. I had grown up thinking I must be a horrible person because I often wished my sister would disappear. I thought I was the only person in the world who felt that way. I also loved my sister and felt protective of her; but because I couldn't talk about the negative feelings, they became exaggerated in my mind. I couldn't make waves, I couldn't get angry and I had no one to talk to. The isolation grew through my childhood.

My recurring dream was a reflection of my feelings; I sat alone in the middle of the ocean.

The need for understanding

The seeds of isolation are sewn early in life if siblings feel excluded from family and other discussions concerning the care of their brother or sister. They often learn indirectly about what is happening in their own family and, as a result, can acquire negative or confused impressions of their situation. Siblings may have difficulty asking questions for fear that they will upset their parents. Victoria, whose younger brother has Down Syndrome, describes how she went through a gradual process of gaining awareness.

> **As a child, I was not fully aware of my brother's disability, limitations. I just thought all boys were the way my brother was. I remember the whispers, and hushed conversations of adults (friends and family), out of my parents' earshot, talking about my brother. I picked up the negativity, secrecy and shame associated with my brother's disability; I didn't really understand it on an intellectual level, but rather felt it on an emotional level.**

Growing up with a sibling with a disability can result in all sorts of confusing feelings. Rachel, in her mid-thirties with two older sisters who have intellectual disabilities, explains that it can be difficult for a young child to understand.

> **Living with a sibling with a disability makes for a *lot* of confusing feelings and issues, which we can only address as adults, when we hopefully have the cognition and tools to**

> **deal with this stuff. There is still a large part of me that responds as a child sometimes. It's like I have an intellectual level of understanding as an adult now, but the emotional level of a child.**

Parents sometimes have difficulty talking about what is happening because of their own emotions. Or they have difficulty saying certain words. Their own information may not be clear and their uncertainty can increase anxiety in other children. Nance talks of her lack of knowledge and difficulties in talking with her mother.

> **My brother was 18 months old when he became gravely ill. Repeated epileptic grand mal fits left him in hospital for months. My mother watched her once joyous little boy whittle away as his brain became irreparably damaged. He also caught the measles at some stage and this exacerbated the intellectual disability. Even now I am not sure of the exact nature of the illness that left my beloved brother the way he is today. Every time I ask my mum it is just too upsetting for her. This means very few conversations take place about my brother and his condition.**

Parents may go through a period of denial, which can be a healthy coping mechanism if it doesn't continue for too long. If parents continue to deny the reality of the situation, siblings can learn to mistrust their own observations and reactions, adding to their confusion and isolation. In extreme cases, these children can become insecure in their own abilities and may learn to rely on others to make decisions, even into adulthood.

Fears and worries

When a child lacks understanding he or she can develop a range of fears and worries. Children may fear that they too have a disability or might develop one down the track. They don't have a clear understanding of how the human body functions, and may worry whenever they become ill that this will lead to a disability similar to that of their brother or sister. Such unexpressed fears can isolate siblings further. Eliza, now in her late twenties, worried as a little girl that she might develop the same 'retardation' as her brother.

> **Especially since the cause of my brother's retardation was unknown, I would think, 'Is this a sign? Is there something wrong with me?'**

Rachel feared that she might have the same problem as her sister.

> **When I was growing up I sometimes thought I actually had what my sib had, just in a milder form. Intellectually I knew that wasn't true, but emotionally – yikes!**

Another sibling grew up with an unusually shaped little finger, which she was sure was a sign that there was something 'wrong' with her as well as her brother.

Some children worry that they may have caused their sibling's disability, especially if the disability develops at a later stage and not at birth. Children don't understand the limits of their powers. A secret wish that their sibling might 'get lost' – a quite normal reaction with children – could be the source of huge amounts of guilt if that brother or sister subsequently becomes ill or develops a disability.

Tara remembers her brother's first seizure.

> **He was playing with my hat and then went very quiet under the dinner table. There was such a panic in the house – it was Christmas lunch. I never let my brother play with anything of mine after that – it was an obsession – in case it caused another seizure.**

Siblings can worry about the safety of a brother or sister and whether they might die. Trips to hospital can be particularly stressful times for a sibling, especially if they are not fully informed about what is happening.

Many siblings talk of a fear of failure, of letting others down. They may worry they will disappoint their parents, who they see as already having enough to deal with. They might therefore constantly seek their parents' approval. Most children will feel safe taking risks and trying new things; if they 'stuff up' they learn to try again and develop perseverance and confidence. Siblings may grow up in a situation where they are not given room to fail. They may feel they have to make up for the limitations of a brother or sister with special needs, or they may feel their own failures will add to the burden or pain of their parents. They may try to meet the needs of parents instead of their own needs. There can be a sense of needing to walk on eggshells in order to avoid adding to the disharmony of the household. The fear of failing, of letting others down, can become too much. The day-to-day stresses can build up and contribute to longer-term anxiety.

Tara talks of her perfectionism.

> **For me the sense of failure at even the smallest mistakes is overwhelming. I attempted suicide at 19 (the first of three attempts). I always felt I had to make up for my brother's inadequacies.**
>
> **Some of my perfectionism is caught up with my guilt; trying to make up for my brother and also trying to make my mother feel better.**

Josie, who is in her early twenties and has a younger brother with cerebral palsy and intellectual disabilities, also talks of the pressure to be perfect.

> **I was the 'good' child. I was told I was good every day of my life. Telling a child what a good child they are, what an angel they are, how wonderful they are to their parents and sibling, causes that child some stress in that they (or at least, I) became scared to disappoint anyone. I lived my life as the perfect child, and boy did that put pressure on me. I used to worry (and occasionally still do) about dying young and then my parents would have no 'normal' children. I was this little eight-year-old worrying about dying and leaving my parents and brother alone.**

Children such as Josie can grow up lacking confidence in themselves and their ability to make decisions on their own. Siblings may also bring that same need for approval into other aspects of their life, particularly a work environment.

Some siblings, in an effort to assuage their guilt, become super-helpful in their homes. If this is kept in balance such contributions can add to a child's sense of competence. But the responsibility to make things right can be too much for a child. Meagan, in her early twenties, spent much of her time caring for a younger brother.

> **My main concern was to stop my family arguing (from stress) and to help with my brother as much as I could to reduce my parents' stress.**

Siblings can also develop fears if their brother or sister is placed in an institution. As well as feeling guilty about not helping enough or perhaps being responsible for the parents' decision, siblings may also fear being 'sent away' if they, too, become a problem for their parents.

A different life

Many adult siblings say, 'If only I could have talked about my feelings with someone who was in the same situation. I would have understood that I wasn't alone.' Few siblings have the opportunity to meet with other children who are in the same situation, but they know their lives are quite different to those of their friends.

At home they may be trying to be special, to be noticed, to be valued. At school and in other social settings, they may be trying to be like everyone else, not to be different or stand out from others. Most times it is difficult for siblings to talk to friends about what it is like to have a brother or sister with disabilities, as they feel their friends may not understand.

Lenore, now in her twenties, whose older brother has intellectual disabilities, autism and epilepsy, realised early that her experience was very different to that of her peer group.

> **I look at the world quite differently from my friends, who have no experience of being a sib. As I put it once, 'normal' family life and parenting is a country I will never be able to visit and whose language I will never understand. My experience just doesn't compute. When my non-sib friends talk about their childhoods, I stay silent for the most part because even when I tell them the bare facts about my brother, the facts can't convey the anguish, resentment, the fear, and everything else mixed in; the childhood experiences I never got to have or were ruined by my brother's outbursts. There's no way they will ever comprehend.**

Tara, also in her twenties, whose younger brother had childhood epilepsy and chronic illness which resulted in physical disability, also felt different when growing up.

> **I never had close friends as a child. My life was so different, I couldn't find a common ground. My family and their needs were the centre of my world. As an adult I still struggle with this sense of loss.**

Eliza was unable to share her experience with others. She felt her experience to be so different that no one could possibly understand.

> **My brother used to keep us up all night with crying and tantrums. He would lay down on the floor in front of my parents' bedroom and kick at their door with his feet while screaming for hours on end. We were all supposed to just get up the next day and go to work or school and never have any outlet for what we experienced all night at home.**

At the age of nine, Lily, who has an older brother with autism, is well aware of her different situation.

> **My brother always makes my life hard and I feel different to everyone else. He's always spitting and he rips up books and sometimes he rips up my homework and I have to do it all again. Not everyone has a brother with autism who does those things. They might have a brother who rips up things but he can talk to them; my brother can't talk to me. Other kids feel 'who really cares?' They think I am making it all up.**

Society's message

Society in general relays the message that those who have a disability in the family should react positively to the situation and feel blessed that they have a 'special' family member. In the media the portrayal of living with a disability is often much removed from the reality. This can make siblings feel even worse about their mixed feelings. Eliza was unable to relate to the media portrayals of families with disability.

> **Sometimes I feel so alone in the negative feelings I have about my disabled sib. I have had almost no opportunities to speak with any other siblings of people with disabilities. The only feedback I ever heard from the world in general while growing up was through sappy after-school TV specials where the sib waxes lyrical about how her disabled sib 'taught her the true meaning of love or courage' . . . or whatever cliché you want to insert here. My sibling taught me the true meaning of frustration!**

Lenore also lacked the opportunities to talk about what was happening in her life.

> **None of the family images I saw in the media showed the reality of life in my house – 12 hours straight of my brother's autistic tantrums, violence, screaming, and then being expected to go to school as if nothing was wrong and never telling anyone at school how much I dreaded going home.**

For families, such media portrayals reinforce the idea that other people don't understand and don't want to know the reality of living day-to-day in a family with disability.

I remember my mother giving me a magazine article to read. It was written by the older brother of a girl with Down Syndrome who lived away from home in an institution. He saw her rarely but his description of one meeting was full of affection, caring and inspiration. He talked about all the gifts she had given him. My mother thought I would be able to relate to his feelings but, instead, reading his tribute made me feel totally inadequate. My experience and feelings were far removed from his. It made any communication about my real feelings even less likely, and reinforced my belief that I was different to every other sibling.

Kerry, in her late twenties and with a younger brother with autism, had an experience closer to mine.

> **I have never felt positively about having a disabled sib. I've accepted it and I've accepted my brother for who he is but his disability will never be a source of inspiration for me. He has accomplished a lot and I'm proud of what he's done but that's not the same.**

Siblings are often told how lucky they are to be 'normal'. It can be difficult for a young child to feel lucky all the time – we all have ups and downs and disappointments – and a sibling can feel pressured always to feel positive and deny their true feelings.

On the flip side many siblings do indeed grow up feeling that their family is special and that they have been blessed with a brother or sister with special needs. Family members can be enriched by their experience. However, many siblings find it difficult to read of such experiences when their own lives have been full of fear, anger and isolation. I question the motives of some writers, who seem at times to be determined to find positives wherever they can.

In my own case, I don't think I will ever reach a point where I can say that my sister's sacrifice was worth any gains I might have made. I can accept that I may be more tolerant of differences and more compassionate to those with special needs, but I would gladly trade these traits for a healthy sister. So let's acknowledge the possible gains from having a person with a disability in the family, but not underplay the reality.

The reactions of others

Society might portray the positive side of living with a child with special needs, but the day-to-day experiences of siblings are often different. They see people shrinking away or staring or making derogatory comments. Some people don't know what to say or how to react when confronted with a person with special needs. They might show pity, avoid the subject or have other awkward reactions. In extreme cases, children may not want to play with siblings of children with special needs. Such responses can lead to a reluctance by siblings to discuss, or even acknowledge, their brother or sister, which in turn increases their feelings of difference and isolation.

Renee, now in her late forties, had a younger brother who died in his late teens from Duchenne Muscular Dystrophy. She remembers her own unsuccessful attempts at talking to others about her brother.

> **I tried sometimes when I was younger to talk about it. I remember school dances. I'd be dancing with someone and they'd ask about brothers and sisters. When I said I had a brother, they'd want to know where he lived. If I said the Home for Incurables, they'd be terribly sorry and then the curtain would come down and that was the end of the conversation. So I learned not to talk about it. It was too difficult for other people.**

Other family members, parents or extended family, can add to the pressure on siblings to keep quiet about the situation or their feelings. Renee remembers the messages she was given.

> **It was never talked about. I recall that I was told that people just progressively get worse and before he was 20 he would die. I was seven at the time. I remember my mother saying, 'You must never tell any other child about this because in a moment of cruelty they will tell your brother he is going to die.' I can understand them saying that but from then on I**

> **never spoke of it and no one ever spoke to me about it. If anyone did, aunts and uncles for instance, it was along the lines of, 'This is a terrible thing your parents have to bear and you must be a good girl for them.' Feelings about the situation were totally suppressed.**

Some parents distance themselves from a sibling through thoughtless comments that come from their own pain. This can add to the child's sense of unworthiness. Fran had to cope with her father, on learning of his only son's disability, saying to her, 'Why couldn't it have been you?' Other siblings have identified similar situations, where a father resents a daughter for being 'normal' when an only son has a disability.

Staring, in particular, can elicit a range of feelings from siblings. Most people don't stare to be cruel. They will have mixed feelings themselves: they might feel uncomfortable, have a sense of pity for the family and also feel lucky they themselves don't need to deal with such difficulties. It might just be natural curiosity.

Young siblings, however, often interpret the stares differently. They often fear that people will think there is something 'wrong' with them, too. At the same time, they might feel overly protective of their brother or sister and be angry with others for staring. It can be especially difficult if a child appears quite 'normal' but behaves in socially unacceptable ways.

Tim, 16, has a younger brother with intellectual disabilities. He says:

> **We always have lots of people who stare at my brother and the rest of our family. Funnily enough it is elderly people who tend to blatantly stare somewhat disapprovingly. My friends tend to accept my brother pretty well but strangers obviously don't know about him, as he doesn't have any obvious physical differences. Some people assume he is just a badly behaved child and make their disapproval quite clear, especially to Mum. This does get me wound up and in a bad mood sometimes.**

Derogatory labels can also upset siblings. I remember that I cringed every time I heard the words 'retards' or 'Mindas' – terms commonly used where I lived as taunts in childhood teasing. (Minda Incorporated provides accommodation and employment for people with intellectual disabilities in South Australia.) I sometimes thought I should try to stop others from using such language and felt inadequate when I didn't. Other siblings are quicker to point out the inappropriateness and in the process teach many lessons.

Young siblings will usually be very protective of their brother or sister and feel hurt and anger when others tease or ridicule. At times, however, they experience conflicting loyalties between family and friends, and may join in with the teasing. This can lead to extreme guilt. It is difficult always to make a stance with others, and the conflicting loyalty adds to the siblings' isolation – they are not quite in either camp.

Pre- and early-school-age children can be more accepting than older children of differences and may not have concerns themselves about what their brother or sister can or cannot do. I've heard parents say that their other children don't fully realise that a brother or sister has a disability, that they treat him or her as 'normal'. It can be tempting for parents to encourage that thinking. There will come a time, however, when others notice the differences. There may be teasing, sniggers or jokes.

Siblings will become aware of others' reactions but may be unprepared and not know how to respond. It will increase their sense of being different if the situation is not explained carefully to them.

Feelings turned inward

The result of all these factors is that children learn that talking about their situation is unacceptable. They may feel confused, yet be too afraid to ask questions. They may develop irrational fears that they cannot understand, let alone express. Siblings may begin to believe that their own feelings are different to everyone else's. As their sense of isolation grows, their feelings can turn inward, creating anxiety and low self-esteem. The next two chapters explore further these difficult feelings and how they might show up in a child's behaviour.

Summary

- Many siblings of children with special needs grow up feeling isolated.
- They can lack understanding of what is happening around them.

- They can develop fears and worries that isolate them further.
- They can feel that their lives are very different from those of peers.
- They are often given the message that they should feel lucky or special. However, others' reactions can increase a sibling's feeling of difference and isolation.

Key strategies to deal with these issues

- Information about a brother's or sister's special needs – see page 152.
- Communication about feelings – see pages 154–162.
- Dealing with others' reactions – see pages 168–170.
- Sibling groups – see pages 172–177.

4

Getting a fair go

> **My life was always made to suit his needs. Never the other way around. It's such a complex thing for a child to grasp.**
>
> – *Renee*

Siblings can grow up with a real sense of unfairness. Life seems to revolve around the child with special needs. Family activities are disrupted. A sibling may not be able to spend time alone with parents. The child with a disability has a greater need for care and attention, but is also often allowed to behave in ways that the sibling is not. Siblings can feel that they are not as important, especially when their achievements attract less fuss than those of the child with a disability. Resentment can develop, possibly leading to a child adopting disruptive behaviours or becoming withdrawn.

What about me?

Young children have difficulty understanding why a brother or sister with special needs is showered with attention. To adults, it is a practical necessity. To a young sibling, attention is linked to love, and it is easy for them to think that their brother or sister with a disability is more important.

Nine-year-old Jordan, when referring to his parents and sister with special needs, says:

> **They like her better than me and always will. They buy her things all the time but not me. All they ever worry about is *her*.**

As one father explained, 'The other children often feel that the child with the disability is more special. My daughter was really happy when she had to have her tonsils out (until she had them out!), and it was because *she* was special.'

Nine-year-old Lily, who has an older brother with autism, says:

> **He gets lots of attention. Sometimes in the middle of dinner he needs to go to the toilet or my parents will need to do something else with him. And I'm just sitting at the table waiting for my sweets and I just have to wait until they're finished. It can be ages.**
>
> **And they buy him lots of new toys to stop him spitting and it's not fair.**

I must have been conscious of attention at an early age. Apparently, when I was quite small I would sometimes refuse to dress myself, even though I was quite capable of doing so. Having watched my mother dress my sister, I would say, 'You dress her, you can dress me!'

My sister seemed to get so much more of my mother's time. She was washed, dressed, fed, put to bed, and if she cried she usually got what she wanted. She would be collected in a big special bus to be taken to her special school. I resented the fact that she got so much attention. I desperately wanted the same.

However, when I did get attention, it was almost too much for me to handle. I felt guilty because I believed that Helen needed it more than me and that really I shouldn't be getting it after all. Seeking attention and then getting it became all jumbled up in a range of emotions that I did not understand. I learnt that to seek attention was somehow bad. I still struggle with that.

When the needs of others come first

Many adult siblings say they grew up feeling abandoned or neglected. In many cases, even the most loving of parents are so stretched by caring for the child with special needs that there is little left for anyone else. Siblings often feel that their needs are put on the back-burner; they feel invisible and uncared for. Parents may be going through their own trauma and be unavailable to able siblings.

Stuart Silverstein is a paediatrician in the United States. His younger brother, Marc, has autism. Together with Bryna Siegel, a developmental psychologist, he wrote *What About Me? Growing up with a developmentally disabled sibling*. In this book, he talks about attention issues.

> **I was four when the severity of his [my brother's] condition was unfolding. At this crucial juncture, when I needed my parents for my own growth and development, they were drowning emotionally while the severity of Marc's condition was becoming apparent . . . There was little, if any, room left over for me and my problems. I was an emotional orphan.**

Rachel talks of the need to take care of herself.

> **I had a happy childhood overall, my parents did their best, but at some level I felt neglected. My parents couldn't help it. I was such a relief to them because I could take care of myself. And they let me look after myself more and more. I used reading a lot to escape. I'm glad I didn't look to drugs and alcohol as an escape.**
>
> **When my counsellor initially suggested I was 'neglected' as a child, I was so appalled. How could anyone think that of *my* parents? Especially knowing what my parents had gone through raising two disabled daughters and then me. But hearing that opinion from someone I trusted and who was objective, did get me thinking and I have realised that it *is* true to some extent . . . maybe not in the traditional sense, but neglect just the same.**

One sibling's mother said, 'I'm glad you're normal so you can take care of yourself.' Some siblings say they felt they were not allowed ever to have problems, and so were left to deal with their issues alone. Not wanting to bother parents who have enough to deal with is a common theme.

Missi, now in her early twenties and with an older sister who is totally dependent on others for her care, became self-reliant.

> **When I was a kid I would be playing outside all day and when I got hurt or had my feelings hurt I felt like I couldn't go to my parents. They had so much work to do with my sister as it was. I took care of myself.**

Later in life it may be difficult for siblings to accept help from others, because they have been so self-sufficient. They may be available to help everyone else but can't allow others to care for them. Some siblings say they can stick up for others, but don't feel that they themselves deserve the same. When needs are negated through childhood it is easy for children to start to trivialise their own needs, and this can continue into adulthood.

Missi continues:

> **I have a lot of trouble showing emotion. I don't cry, I don't get upset. I don't always feel normal either. I feel like I am too nice and people walk all over me. I always seem to put other people first and think of myself as lesser, which isn't healthy, but I do it anyway.**

Renee, too, felt that her needs always came second and that she was never as important as her brother.

> **Because muscular dystrophy is progressive, my brother could still walk until he was seven. When he started school my parents wanted him to go to a school that was closer and so *I* had to change schools to the one he went to. It made sense but it became in my mind an example to me of how my life was always made to suit his needs.**

Fran, whose younger brother has Down Syndrome, says:

> **Everyone knew me as Geoffrey's sister. No one said, 'Oh, you're Fran, you've got pretty blonde hair.' It was all about him. I was always a bit of a nobody.**

Lenore says:

> **I feel such frustration with my parents' attitude that my disabled sibling must be considered at *all costs*. It affected their health and contributed to my mother's premature death. My whole life until age 18 was forcibly constrained around 'Don't upset your brother', 'Don't argue', 'He can't help it'. He regularly broke my belongings and tried to kill me, and my parents let him do it, let him rule the house and rule my life and all our lives because they were afraid and guilty and compassionate and I don't know what else.**

Often more fuss is made of the achievements of the child with special needs. Siblings can begin to doubt their own worth, to feel that they are 'not quite good enough'. Gina certainly felt the differences.

> I always knew that my parents cared a lot for me but in so many ways they gave the message that my sister was superior in her claims upon their attention. It was so easy to think, 'Well, what's wrong with me if they care to give so much attention to *her* – there's something wrong here.'

Putting others' needs first can lead to unhealthy relationships, as Nance explains.

> I realise now that being the 'giver' and 'peacemaker' in the family has affected my relationships with the opposite sex. I look back now on many of the relationships I've had with boys and realise that I was too willing to take on the giving, nurturing role, to a degree where I was taken advantage of. I had grown up in an environment where, despite my parents trying to do their best for my brother without limiting me, all the family decisions were based on whether he could cope, and what he wanted. Many times I remember we had to cancel family get-togethers because my brother threw a tantrum. There was no way to reason with him when he became like that. The pattern of putting another person before yourself all the time became ingrained. I gave too much of myself to boyfriends and was too willing to acquiesce to their sometimes ridiculous demands. I thought that was what you did in life. I now realise that my brother's needs are exceptional and I have a different set of limitations for the other people in my life. But this took a long time to learn.

Tara also now understands the effects of suppressed emotions on her relationships with others.

> At 28, I have just realised that I do not know how to relate to others unless I can identify something that they need from me. My own needs are hidden even from myself and occasionally brought to the surface through anger. I wonder what it is to cry.

A lack of time with parents

Some activities may not be possible for families that include a child with a disability. Holidays, going out to dinner or other entertainment might be too difficult. As Julie says:

> We didn't do much as a family in the way of holidays and other activities, though I didn't feel at the time that I missed

> **out on anything. Now that I have my own family, I realise the restrictions that affected us then.**

Josh, who is 11 and has a younger sister with special needs, says: 'I wish I could do things with Mum and Dad but I can't – I could before *she* was born.'

Lenore says:

> **I downplayed anything I did well that might require parental attendance, because my brother would have to be taken along, and he would invariably throw an autistic/psychotic tantrum and have to be removed. As a result, I didn't ask my parents to attend when I was in choral performances or theatre or the like, or just said that I understood they couldn't come because of my brother.**

Simultaneously, siblings may long to spend time with their parents. Tara yearned to be with her mother.

> **There were times at night when I would listen to my mother read to my brother in the next room. I would hear the machinery helping him to breathe and tense at every break in the rhythm. I was not allowed to go into his room at those times. I suppose Mum thought she was protecting me. In reality I would curl into a small ball and cry endlessly, wishing myself far away, wishing for Mum to read to *me*, wishing for a time where I could be special and hugged and wanted around.**

'Single' siblings often experience the strange combination of feeling like an only child, but missing out on the attention that an only child often receives. At the same time they often feel compelled to take on a 'second mother' role to their sibling.

The relationship with the primary caregiver

An important part of child development involves early attachment to a significant adult. This enables a child to develop a strong sense of self and to be able, as time goes on, to form healthy relationships with others.

Sometimes these processes can be disrupted when a child in the family has special needs. An able child may have had a secure attachment to his mother, but, with the subsequent birth of a child with special needs, he may suffer a sense of abandonment as his mother devotes much time and energy to the new child. (The primary caregiver is usually the mother but could just as easily be a father or other adult.)

If the able child is born after the child with special needs, the mother may still be dealing with issues of loss and this can affect the relationship with the able child. One mother, who had two daughters with intellectual disabilities and then went on to have another daughter, spoke in later years to her able daughter. She confided how low her self-esteem had been after having her first two children. She went on to say, 'You were the perfect baby, you responded to me just like you should, I had to protect myself from loving you too much.'

A mother's preoccupation with the child with special needs, combined with her own mixed feelings (guilt, sorrow, anger) about what is happening in her life, may lead to her not being able to give her able child what she needs to develop a sense of security. Without that, a child is likely to develop a range of fears and anxieties.

Part of a child developing security involves feeling that she can rely on a primary caregiver to be there for her. Children can usually 'test the water' and take risks – by misbehaving, yelling at their mother, telling her in anger that they hate her – knowing that the relationship is strong enough to withstand them. In a family with a child with a disability, a sibling may feel less important and feel that the relationship with her mother is not strong enough to risk such behaviour.

A secure child will know that a mother, for example, can handle these threats; that she is strong enough to deal with such behaviour. A mother of a child with special needs may appear more fragile to an able child. She may be depressed or stressed from the day-to-day caregiving required for a child with special needs.

Some siblings say they never rebelled or tested the limits during their adolescence, again protecting parents from further distress.

The attractions of a disability

To a child, the idea of disability actually holds some attractions. The child with a disability seems to get special treatment, and not only within the family. Gina expressed it in the following way:

People would come to visit and they would say, 'I brought a present for your sister because she's deaf. You understand don't you?' I would smile and nod and say yes. But I resented it. And I can remember the look on my mother's face and the words she used when one day I said quite definitely, 'I wish I was deaf.' She quietly said, 'You don't,' but I *did*. Right then and there I wanted to be deaf because if you were deaf, people gave you so much and when there were six kids there wasn't a lot to go around.

There were so many things she had that I couldn't have, but wanted. I understood that she had to have those things – well, sort of. I would have loved to have had a warm dressing gown to put on in the mornings to keep me warm but I didn't have one. She had to have one though, because she was deaf. In reality, she needed one to take to boarding school where she went during the week, but the message I was given was that she had to have a gown because *she's deaf*. I really wanted the things she had.

At Christmas time she would get the slightly better presents. One Christmas we received dolls and she had the one with the opening and closing, beautiful, glassy blue eyes and I had a solid bloody thing whose arms and legs wouldn't move. All these little things meant such a lot to a child of six or seven. I felt the pain so often and thought, 'It's not fair.'

Years later, as an adult, I realised that I no longer resented her, and hadn't done so for a long time. I realised that my life was so much better – how could I have resented her? But as a child the understanding is not there.

Renee's brother was confined to a wheelchair.

There was a certain amount of attraction about the wheelchair. I remember going to a football match once with my family and strangers would come up to my brother in his wheelchair and give him lollies or money. I'd look sideways and think, 'Well, why aren't I getting those?' There was a certain appeal because he got all the attention.

The one relative I really loved as a child was my maternal grandfather. When he visited, at some stage he would always take me aside quietly and give me a pound note, which was a large amount in those days. He'd say, 'It's *just* for you, don't tell anybody.' And it was the only example

I can think of where someone selected me for no apparent reason at all.

I was a fairly quiet, shy child but the attention-seeking was there in almost every aspect of my life – in the home, in relation to outsiders and relatives. I wanted something I couldn't have, because I wasn't special in any way.

Again, the sibling can experience inner conflict as she strives to let people know that she isn't like her brother, while at the same time perhaps wanting to be like her brother to ensure some special attention.

'Acting up' to gain attention

Some children will misbehave in order to attract attention. Victoria reflects that she would get into trouble regularly so that her parents would notice her.

As a child either I would attempt to fade into the background and take care of myself or, when the need for parenting was overwhelming, I would attract negative attention. As I heard a psychologist say, 'Children would rather be praised than punished, but they would rather be punished than ignored.' So I would act up.

It can be difficult for parents, under stress themselves, to understand that such negative behaviour is a result of the stresses the child is experiencing. Of course, not all children act up. Some manifest other behaviours that may also be signs of distress.

Being perfect to gain attention

Many siblings talk of an internal pressure to succeed as a way of attracting attention. Renee felt the push to get good grades.

In reality there is no energy left for the other child, so much is needed for the disabled one. I learnt fairly early on that the only way to get attention was to have good grades at school. The only thing I ever got attention for was the good report card that was brought home. So you put a whole lot of energy into that. That's what my parents saw and what I got praised for. In every other aspect of life they were directing their energies elsewhere.

Tara adds:

> **I got positive attention from my mother when I did excel – academically or in a public forum. But so much of my mother's attention was focused on my brother that even when I did achieve high grades, or received dancing or academic awards, I never felt good enough.**

For some siblings the urgent need to succeed may derive from an attempt to compensate their parents for their sibling with a disability, who won't necessarily achieve the same feats. They see the pain in their parents and want to make them proud. They may be conscious of how lucky they are and feel they must make the most of the abilities they have. Many siblings feel they never quite meet the expectations of their parents or extended family and many struggle with the fear of letting people down, or disappointing them. There is a danger that such a child will feel unworthy without constant success. But even when successful, these siblings often still feel unworthy.

As Nance says:

> **I felt a huge responsibility to my parents, even more than to myself, to be successful at whatever I did, so they could have a child they could feel proud of. Not that they weren't proud of my brother, but I knew that being the only 'normal' child, to a degree all their hopes and dreams for both their children were somehow sitting on my shoulders. I realise all too much that I am the only child who will be able to provide them with the joy of grandchildren.**

Tara still struggles with the pressures.

> **I danced from the age of four and was always expected to be the best. When I was injured in my early teens I felt so guilty that I competed anyway and now have lifelong chronic pain in my back and knees; I just couldn't let my mother down. As a young adult I had to achieve academically. I remember telling my father I wanted to work in retail and his words were 'I am so disappointed that you would give up your dreams of study and high achievement.' Needless to say, I returned to university and am now completing post-graduate work. I have so internalised the need to achieve and be the best I can be for my family that I feel jealous of my brother's achievements.**

Perhaps that is because my achievements are met with comments about the 'next step' while his are met with joy at the individual achievement's merit. I often feel I can never be good enough, never achieve enough, never make up for my family's pain. Sadly, I am still trying at 28.

The pressure may come from parents who openly push their other children to succeed in ways the child with a disability cannot. Some parents don't exert pressure, but gain pleasure from seeing their child's successes, in spite of the family difficulties. On the other hand, some parents try to discourage their other children, perhaps through a fear that their achievements will show up the more minor successes of the child with a disability. Or they may want their other children to keep their aspirations low because of their own disappointments. Victoria felt that her parents actually discouraged her.

I felt that my parents did not see me as an intelligent young woman, but rather as one who should keep her expectations and aspirations low. I assume that I was being discouraged primarily because they were so disappointed with my brother's condition that they never wanted to be disappointed again, nor did they want me to suffer disappointment as great as theirs.

It's not fair!

Siblings often see the child with a disability getting away with inappropriate behaviour and not being held responsible for anything. On the other hand, the sibling is made to behave and often has to take on extra responsibilities, such as helping the parents care for the child with special needs. As an adult it is easy to understand why this is so, but as a child it may not make sense.

It is difficult for parents to treat their able and disabled children equally. Often they acknowledge they let their child with a disability behave in ways that their other children cannot. Often they feel the child with a disability asks for so little, they should get what they want. Sometimes it is difficult to know what are appropriate limits for a child with special needs. Rachel's mother explained it to her, as an adult, in the following way:

I know you used to get mad at me for not telling your sisters when they did something wrong, but if you correct someone on something and they learn from it, then it is an appropriate

> **thing to do. But if they don't learn from it, and you tell them over and over and over again and they still don't learn . . . Well, I had to let go sometime, because if I kept correcting them and correcting them and correcting them again, then their whole lives would have been filled up with negativity and I didn't want that for them.**

Having this conversation with her mother forced Rachel to reassess her beliefs and realise that she had little understanding of the situation as a child.

Like most siblings, my sister and I fought, sometimes physically. She was very strong in one arm and would often hit me. If I retaliated, I was told, 'Don't do that. She can't help it.' It seemed so unfair. Sometimes the child with a disability has a particular way of behaving that shuts off responsibility. Gina talks of her frustration at not being able to fight back.

> **My sister would say something mean to me, but if I attempted to retaliate, she would shut her eyes. That was it, I couldn't do anything. It was so frustrating because she could get me, she could hurt me any time she wanted and I couldn't retaliate in kind.**

Many siblings talk of their frustration at parents 'spoiling' a child with special needs. A sibling may have felt that the child with special needs was indeed able to understand what was right and wrong. A sibling might also feel that the child with special needs could have been encouraged to contribute to the household in simple ways that would have helped the child develop more independence.

Siblings often end up with a chip on their shoulder. Life can seem so unfair, even with the most loving and caring parents. As adults, it is easier to see the need for the differences and understand that love is not necessarily related to attention. As children, however, the perceived injustice can lead to anger and resentment, and then it is difficult to know where to direct those feelings.

Summary

- Siblings can miss out on attention from parents.
- Siblings can learn to put the needs of others before their own.
- At times they may wish they too had special needs.
- They may act up in order to gain attention.

- They may feel pressure to be perfect in order to gain attention and to make things right for parents.
- They may feel resentment that the child with special needs is being spoiled, that she is being treated differently and being allowed to get away with inappropriate behaviour.

Key strategies to deal with these issues

- Communication within the family – see pages 150–160.
- Helping siblings feel valued – see pages 162–164.
- Acknowledging and valuing the care given by siblings – see pages 164–165.

5

Feelings with nowhere to go

> **I'm always being nice to people, even when I should be more demanding. It's hard for me to show my feelings, and when I do and someone feels hurt, I'm overcome with guilt. I never get angry. –** ***Tara***

Siblings often sense that it is not acceptable for them to talk about their feelings in relation to their brother or sister. If left unexpressed, emotions such as anger, embarrassment, fear and guilt can build up and contribute to ongoing anxiety, shame, low self-esteem and possibly depression. Some of this distress can also show up as behavioural problems. The stories that follow show how the experiences of sibling children can manifest as emotional problems in adulthood.

Anger

As a child I felt much anger: at my sister for being the way she was; at my parents for the special treatment they gave her; at everyone else for staring and not understanding. This anger had to be hidden; there was nowhere to direct it, so it turned in on me. I became self-doubting and frustrated at my perceived inadequacies.

If I did ever show anger toward my sister by lashing out physically, I was told that she couldn't help hurting me and so I shouldn't hurt her. I needed to have my own hurt acknowledged as well. Over time I had difficulty learning to stand up for myself.

There are several reasons why siblings find it difficult to express their anger and frustration. If you feel sorry for someone, it can be difficult to show anger toward them.

As well as feeling sorrow for a sibling with a disability, children often feel sorry for their parents and want so much to make things right for them. It can be difficult for children to express anger toward parents whom they see as dealing with enough stress already. Many adult siblings say that they still struggle with anger and need counselling to help them learn to express it and deal with it.

In his book *What About Me? Growing up with a developmentally disabled sibling*, Stuart Silverstein writes about denial.

> In reading through the essays and stories written by other siblings of handicapped children, I see a similar tendency toward a denial of their feelings. Instead, they acknowledge the more positive emotions and experiences. They talk about their 'special' brother, how he has brought the family closer together, makes them laugh, and makes them so much more compassionate. Everyone then steps back and says, 'Now isn't that nice. His sister has adjusted so well to the situation.' I see very little acknowledgment of the darker emotions. What about the hurt, anger, frustration, and resentment that I know exists? . . . We siblings are not supposed to feel angry and resentful. Such feelings imply selfishness and insensitivity. But in not acknowledging these feelings, we only feed into denial . . .
>
> In the beginning, my denial was so strong that, when asked what impact Marc has had on my life, I proudly claimed, 'Since Marc was around all my life, and as I have never known any different: no impact!' I then explained how much more sensitive to others I am because of Marc. I think that, as a child, I was perceptive enough to realise that this was what others were comfortable hearing. An expression of my true feelings would have been too overwhelming for all concerned.

He goes on to say:

> Denial leaves you out of touch with your true feelings, incapable of finding the necessary energy to deal with the situation at hand. You end up mistrusting your own intuition in important situations and heading down the path to insecurity, low self-esteem, and depression. You are left a legacy of helplessness.

Rachel now understands the difficulty she had in talking about negative feelings in her family and the long-term consequence of that isolation.

> **It is hard for me to say that my parents 'neglected' me because I don't want to add to their burden, but I know in my heart it is true. I often feel that if I had happy things or positive things to express, that was okay, but if I was negative, that wasn't okay.**
>
> **I remember in eighth grade I wrote a poem entitled 'My Name is Rachel and I'm Always Happy'. It was about how everyone always thought I was so happy, and told me all their troubles, but I could never tell anyone mine, and I always did everything with a smile, which masked everything.**

Renee expresses similar sentiments:

> **Parents are involved totally with a seriously ill or disabled child. They also get a chance to talk to each other. Especially if you are the only other child, there is no one to talk to. It would have been difficult to get me to articulate my feelings. I was trying so hard to be the 'good' child. It seems that the child who appears to be unaffected by what is happening around them is perhaps the most profoundly affected.**

She was also afraid to show her own vulnerability.

> **By the time I was a teenager I could have discussed it but to me it seemed too difficult. Why would I suddenly want to appear so vulnerable, where maybe I'd cry or whatever?**

Gina is one of six children. Her sister, older by 14 months, is deaf. Even though she had younger siblings, she still had no one to talk to.

> **I had many negative feelings but could not tell anybody else. I would think a lot and it was difficult to express my feelings. I suppressed my feelings for my sister. I couldn't express anger or frustration, except by bursts of fury. Learning to express anger as an adult has taken a long time.**
>
> **I'm also very private because so much of what we did was visible to everyone else. Every time she spoke everyone focused and we were always the centre of everyone else's**

> attention. When she wasn't there I was left very much to my own thoughts and feelings, and went inside myself for support.
>
> I had learnt from a young age not to react, not show emotion on my face. It taught me a lot of control. I could mask everything if I wanted to. You should be able to acknowledge what you are thinking and feeling, verbalise and deal with it. But I couldn't do that. You sacrifice all your thoughts and feelings to the needs of the other person.

Tara also felt isolated.

> I felt totally alone at times in my family. My mother protected my brother from the world with a ferociousness that scared me. I was conscious that my father's attempts to nurture me caused conflict between him and Mum. By the time I was 12 I was bulimic; 14, anorexic; 19, clinically depressed. I turned my feelings of anger, hurt, isolation and loneliness upon myself. At 28 I can finally recognise this – it feels like a long road ahead.

Carly describes her own spiral toward an eating disorder and depression.

> I grew up in an isolated part of the country. My sister is five years older and my brother, who has severe epilepsy and a mild intellectual disability, is three years older than me. As a child, he spent many months of every year hospitalised, which meant he and my mother were not home for extended periods of time.
>
> I felt I had to be the perfect child and not cause my family any problems. I was expected to be the child who would make something of my life and go on to university. My sister acted up and rebelled as a teenager but I was told not to turn out like her. I never felt good enough.
>
> In addition to the pressure to be perfect, I grew up with a lack of attention. I felt my life was put on hold until my brother left home at 16 to attend a special school. Suddenly my life started again. Attention was poured on me as though I was a five-year-old child; but I was 13 and the attention was too late. I needed it when I was younger. In some ways, I wanted to stay a child.

> I held a lot of resentment for all my family, including constant thoughts as a child of wishing my brother was dead.
>
> At the age of 15, I developed an eating disorder – anorexia nervosa – and severe depression. I have no doubt, looking back, that a major contributing factor was the feelings that developed around having a disabled brother.

Looking at what contributes to an eating disorder is complex. For Tara and Carly, it seemed to spring from internalising feelings, a lack of nurturing and self-abuse. Others might develop an eating disorder as a way of gaining some control over their lives, where as a sibling they have grown up with little control over their external environment. For others, symptoms can be related to the pressure of trying to be perfect.

Many siblings talk of their concern for parents and how this inhibits their expression of feelings. Renee explains:

> One of my hesitations with talking to you for this book was that you might identify me and I would be worried about the effect on my parents. It's a protective thing. Anger, et cetera, can't spill out onto your parents. In the overall scheme of things the much greater loss was theirs.
>
> Ever since my brother died we've had Christmas at our place. I have had anger about that. Why do I always have to be the parent? I went away a couple of times. I felt it was cruel, but I needed to.
>
> There is so much to work through at a later age. You need to do it all at an accelerated rate. In some ways you have to be a child again at 40. You can say that it's ridiculous to be jealous of your sibling, but you are. And you say to yourself, 'Gee, I'm not like this in any other area of my life.'

Julie, also in her forties, commented that any effects on her were nothing compared to what her parents went through.

> I think there is a lot of repressed anger. With my mother in particular, I have always been too afraid to show too much anger, because I think she's had enough to deal with. So I don't think you ever get it out. It probably never gets resolved.

Josie also continues to feel anger toward her parents into adulthood.

I have spent 24 years as a parent pleaser. It used to be that I felt guilty if I ever thought something negative about my parents, let alone say it out loud! I would think, 'How dare I say something bad about my mum and dad when they have had to deal with all this stuff.' When my friends complained about their mums, I never said a word. Whenever I say something negative I feel like I need to also say, '*But* they are wonderful parents and I'm very close to them', 'I couldn't ask for better parents' and so on. All of this is true, *but* I can never say a negative without adding a positive.

I am finally being honest about my feelings in regards to my mum and dad. Now that I am older I am starting to realise that I can love someone with all of my heart and sometimes still be frustrated or angry with them! What a relief that has been for me.

For Rachel, marriage was the catalyst for understanding and change.

Being in a marriage forced me to deal with things. In most other relationships, if something bothers me, I can just leave for a time, or extricate myself from the situation, but with a spouse, it isn't that easy. I recognised that I couldn't fight with my spouse properly and was holding a lot of anger and resentment toward him for that. Counselling helped a lot.

There can be anger at others, especially those who stare and tease. As a child I would often stare back, and remember wanting to do something like poke my tongue out at them. I'm not sure if I actually did. It was another situation where I couldn't direct my anger specifically at someone. I had to keep it hidden.

Renee had similar reactions.

I can remember walking down the street and people crossing to the other side to avoid us. I remember poking out my tongue at people. One stare and they'd get it from me. Of course, if my parents saw me I'd be in trouble. But it must have been very hard for my parents.

Again, the concern for parents appears to be the overriding factor here.

Depression

Siblings talk about the periods of depression they suffer throughout their lives. Depression often arises in the context of unexpressed anger, or other feelings that have been repressed. One definition of depression is 'anger turned inward', so it's not surprising that siblings can experience depression and low self-esteem. This often goes unnoticed and if young people feel depressed, they may hesitate to express it to their family because their problems feel insignificant alongside the problems of others. They may not be able to talk to people outside the family either, if they are trying to hide the reality of their home life. For some siblings, a sense of helplessness can build up.

Everyone has ups and downs with periods of feeling flat or unhappy. There can be pressures (both external and internal) on siblings to deny these quite normal down times. Constantly trying to be perfect and keeping negative feelings hidden can eventually take their toll.

Rachel recognises the source of her depression.

> **I realise now that if ever I was mad or hurt or angry (especially at my disabled sib), my parents and I just didn't know how to deal with it, so we didn't. All that 'emotion stuffing' has taken a big toll, and I have been on anti-depressants, in counselling and group therapy for several years.**

Tara's inbuilt anger has led to ongoing depression.

> **I am angry so much of the time. Angry at the world for making my life like this, angry at my brother for his disability/health problems. Mostly I am angry at myself for not coping, for not being the perfect daughter, for failing to make life easier and better for everyone.**

Siblings can reach crisis point at varying times. Like me, many siblings talk of it all coming unstuck during their teen years, when emotions can ordinarily seem difficult and confusing. Add to the mix all the issues related to a brother or sister with disabilities and the pressures can become overwhelming. Seventeen-year-old Vera, whose sister has cerebral palsy, describes her struggles with depression.

> **I had bouts of depression for various reasons, mainly through being in a family with a disabled sister – the stress that is present, the feelings that are never mentioned. Recently this depression has grown. It is something that I have to deal with on a daily basis. I get shaky, scared, emotional, withdrawn. It is pretty scary but I am sure it will get better. I used to use school work, real work, organising, planning my life, to withdraw myself. Now I have a lot more fun, I have more of a life, a wonderful boyfriend I love and respect. But sometimes I just can't sleep. I feel like there is this black hole.**

For children who have no other brothers or sisters apart from the child with a disability, the difficulties can be exacerbated. In most families, sisters and brothers provide children with their first social contact. Through this they learn to give and take, to share and to stick up for themselves and for each other. In families where there is more than one sibling without a disability, there are more opportunities to learn these skills. These children also have more of an opportunity to share some of their feelings instead of internalising them. For single siblings, the isolation and self-doubt can be immense.

Lenore highlights a common feeling among siblings who ask, 'Why did this happen to my brother or sister?' but at the same time know there is no answer to the question and nowhere to direct their angst.

> **I keep telling myself that asking 'why?' is pointless at this time in my life; that my energies are better devoted to coping. But there's always that little voice locked away in the back of my mind that wants to rage at the sky.**

Many siblings are able, as adults, to work through the negative feelings and experience relief from depression or other symptoms. Strategies that may help siblings are explored in chapter 9.

Embarrassment

Embarrassment is something siblings can begin to experience as they grow older. Pre-school children may accept a disabled brother or sister completely, and not feel any discomfort. However, embarrassment may come during school years when siblings become more aware of others' reactions.

Victoria saw her classmates making fun of another child with intellectual disabilities.

> **That is when I became ashamed that my brother too was retarded, and I didn't want anyone to know, for fear they would make fun of me. I already had enough going against me. I wore glasses, I was chubby and I was smart; three things that easily killed popularity when you are a child. I didn't need a retarded brother too.**

Embarrassment is what I remember most as a child, and after all these years, it is still there. Wherever we went people stared. Part of me felt protective of Helen, and concerned about how she felt. But most of all, I felt extremely embarrassed. I was terrified that people would think I was like her, that I too was disabled in some way. I wanted to yell at them that I was okay. I always sensed that I was being judged.

My teen years were full of uncertainty. So much of adolescence is about creating an identity. I seemed to be pulled in so many directions. I knew I couldn't use my older sister as my model in trying to form my own identity. I felt a heightened sense of guilt and sorrow when I compared her life to mine. My self-consciousness seemed to blow out of control. Again, I had no one with whom to share my thoughts and feelings. Many siblings say that it was during their teen years in particular that they felt acute embarrassment. Some go through a stage where they don't want to be seen with their brother or sister.

I felt uncomfortable when friends came to dinner. I tried to act cool but my stomach was churning. Helen always struggled with her eating. She had to eat by pushing one mouthful of mashed food down with the next. She would also belch and laugh loudly. And in spite of my mother's efforts, she always smelt of dribble.

I dreaded bringing boyfriends home. I was sure they would feel uncomfortable when they met my sister and that they would lose interest in me. I talked recently to an old boyfriend from my early twenties. He remarked that he wasn't at all disturbed by Helen's behaviour, but could see that I was deeply concerned by it. He said he could never quite understand why.

As soon as I finished university studies I moved into a flat with friends. I needed to get away, to show myself that I could cope on my own. I didn't stay away long, but it was important to have some space away for a while.

When I was about 20 I decided to do something nice for my sister on my own. I took her to the musical *Godspell*, starring John Farnham. Helen was, and still is, a real fan of his. She made her usual noises and I spent the whole show grabbing her arm, pinching it, anything to try and stop her attracting attention to her and to me. I hated the whole outing, and then felt terribly guilty afterwards for not allowing her to enjoy the show.

Renee also felt this heightened sense of conspicuousness.

> **There was embarrassment of the wheelchair, the confinement, the obviousness of it all. My brother was quite large. If he needed to urinate a huge metal bottle would be brought out. I found it mortifying, and didn't know whether to explain or go away.**

For Julie, whose sister suffered mild intellectual disabilities, the embarrassment wasn't huge, but was still there.

> **I used to feel embarrassed when people came home. I would introduce her briefly and then run off to play. I did nothing to include her in our play.**

Nance, like others, avoided bringing friends home.

> **While I was never ashamed of my brother, and most of my friends knew about him, I look back now and realise I rarely took friends home. I always tried to find a way I could go to their place instead. It was only the people I felt I could trust the most that came into my house.**

Gina also felt uncomfortable and feared others would think there was something wrong with her.

> **I can remember being in the shops and my sister was trying to talk to my mother and she couldn't modulate her volume. When deaf children learnt to speak they would look in the mirror, feel their throat and would try to mouth the words in the right way.**
>
> **She was calling out 'Mum'. If you look at the way your lips form she was crying out 'bum, bum' very loudly and everyone was looking at this child who looked perfectly**

normal but who, in those days, was being extremely rude. But no one knew. I felt like saying, 'She's deaf, she doesn't know what she's saying.'

I had to excuse her all the time, explain why she didn't respond to people.

People would stare at her all the time if they couldn't understand her. It made me feel important translating for her. I felt very needed but she had such a loud voice and when we were out people would stare. I felt like saying, 'It's not me, I might be using my fingers, but *I'm* not deaf, I'm not talking like that.' So as well as using my fingers to sign, I would make sure I was talking so people knew I was okay, I was normal. I wasn't the one with the problem.

There were amusing incidents too. One time, as adults, we were at the hairdressers together and we signed. The girls working in the shop presumed we were both deaf and so were talking about us. I was so embarrassed and didn't know what to do. I didn't say a word, though I should have. They chatted away about all sorts of things – not only about us but also about their everyday lives, what they did with boyfriends in the back seat of the car. When we left I thanked them and said I hoped they had a good day. One of them replied, 'Can you hear?' When I replied that I could, her face dropped. Though part of me was amused, I felt very guilty.

Fear

Another emotion experienced by many siblings is fear. Earlier I mentioned the fear of also developing a disability, but other fears are possible as well.

If the child with a disability has extreme behavioural difficulties, siblings may fear for their own safety. Consider the child who locks herself in her room every time her older brother with autism goes 'ballistic', afraid that he will hurt her, break something or at the very least upset her mother. This child is learning to withdraw from stressful situations. This might result in her withdrawing from other aspects of her life.

Another sibling, an adult woman, is still unable to be in the same room as her brother without feeling panic. As a child, she had been on the receiving end of much of her brother's aggressive behaviour. Some children with disabilities can be quite destructive, and this can create anxiety in siblings who may be younger and smaller. Living with such anxiety on a day-to-day basis can lead to longer-term problems with anxiety.

Some siblings have talked of parents not protecting them, even dismissing their fears and placing the blame back on the sibling. Some parents' level of denial of the situation is so strong they don't recognise the dangers. Denial is a coping mechanism, but it can put both the child with special needs and siblings at risk. Of course, some siblings will physically hurt a child with special needs. In some cases, this can add to the guilt they might be feeling already. They need to learn more appropriate ways of dealing with their feelings.

Even parents can experience fear, especially when children reach adolescence and become bigger and stronger. These parents may feel tremendous guilt about feeling such fear, and find it difficult to share the emotion with anyone.

In addition to fears for their own safety, siblings often worry about the safety of a brother or sister with special needs, and feel powerless to help them. Renee talks of a fear that her brother would die.

> **People with muscular dystrophy can die of something minor, like a cold. Several times a year my brother would be rushed to hospital and have his lungs pumped. I remember sitting and waiting, not knowing if he would die. Everyone else was so worried, there was no energy to give to me. There was no chance to talk about my fear or anxiety.**
>
> **A lot of feelings reflected an effort to gain control. I can remember my father telling me that my brother lifting his arm off the table would be as difficult as my trying to lift the piano with a little finger. I had such a sense of absolute powerlessness. When children are growing up, I think you give them a sense of all the things they *can* do, but suddenly, at a very early age, I found there was something absolutely overwhelming about which I could do nothing. It's not a nice thing, either.**
>
> **My husband says that when he first met me I was very pessimistic. If there were two outcomes, I'd always anticipate the worst. My explanation was that something terrible had happened before, so why not again?**

> **In lots of different ways my childhood situation has had adverse effects on me. It still comes back and takes a while to work through and deal with.**

Other siblings have talked of having an awareness at a very young age of the fragility of life. These children are more conscious of what can go wrong and, in the process, miss out on some of the innocence of childhood. They may find it difficult to develop optimism. For some the fear and anxiety can continue through life, and not talking about it adds to the ongoing stress.

Guilt

As a child, if I felt anger or resentment, if I upset my parents, or was having too good a time, I felt guilty. If I wanted my parents' attention, I felt guilty, knowing that my sister needed it more. If I felt embarrassed by her, I also felt guilty.

Helen missed out on so much. I could go to friends' houses, play sport, do ballet. I remember going to birthday parties as a child, leaving my sister crying in the driveway because she could not go too. It was difficult to really enjoy myself. I started to feel guilty about having too much, for living a normal life. It is a kind of 'survivor guilt'. I still find that guilt is an issue. I wonder if Helen thinks I have everything – job, husband, children – and she has so little. I doubt that she does, given her intellectual disability, but it tears me apart to think that she might.

Other siblings have said they can't allow themselves to enjoy good things, that they feel they don't deserve pleasure. They always feel the pain of others: their brother or sister, their parents. Deep down they don't feel they deserve happiness. Rachel has a lot of happiness in her life – a satisfying career, a much-loved husband and a young son – but still struggles with guilt.

> **I struggle with depression and guilt and anger and grief every single day of my life, to the extent that I am on medication. I abuse my body by overeating and not exercising because somewhere deep down in the middle of my being, I know I feel terrible that my siblings have mental retardation and I don't. I still have to work quite a bit on the concept that 'it's okay that I'm okay'.**

American paediatrician Stuart Silverstein writes in his book *What About Me?* about his ambivalence at visiting his brother's group home.

> To see him in the home, I will have to face up to the fact that his life is severely limited, and that he will always be dependent on others. How could I then turn around and enjoy my life, after leaving him behind? As long as I don't have an image of his real world, I can envision it as being as pleasant as I want.

'Survivor guilt' can rob survivors of their future. There is always someone whose pain seems worse. Rachel, who works as an occupational therapist, says:

> I used to have such a hard time dealing with my depression. I would think, 'How can I feel so bad when I work with people with *real* problems?' Or I would think about what my sisters have to deal with and it would just make me feel worse! I have to learn that even though I have a good life and am thankful, I may still feel bad or sad or rotten and it is important to be okay with it.

Renee expresses the desire to be able to feel down at times without feeling bad about it, and to be able to complain without guilt.

> I remember that whenever I'd grumble about anything to my parents they'd say, 'Well you've got your health and you can run around. Be grateful and that (whatever I was grumbling about) is a trivial thing in life.'
>
> Guilt is a very large thing here. I didn't understood it as guilt until I saw the film *Ordinary People*. A brother realises that he feels guilty for surviving when his brother drowns. Once you acknowledge that, it helps.
>
> That guilt carries through in many ways and, for me, it's still there. My son recently had his twenty-first birthday. Not long before that, he had moved out of home and I was missing him terribly. At the party an aunt asked me how I felt about his leaving home and I replied that it was a real trauma adjusting to his absence, that it felt like he'd died. My mother heard me and said, 'Well you shouldn't feel like that, my son did die and I never got to see his twenty-first.'

> I felt angry. I wanted to say that, for once, I'm just talking about how *I* feel. I wanted her to understand that there are other losses in the world besides her great loss as a mother, and that mine didn't need to be compared to hers all the time.
>
> I felt angry, and guilty for enjoying my son's twenty-first, and I shouldn't have had to feel that way. I can now talk with my husband and work through it, but I'm not going to have it out with my mother – it's too difficult.

The guilt can carry through a lifetime. Siblings can struggle with the conflicting feelings of wanting to leave home and gain independence and wanting to support their families. Often they need a reason, like going away to university, getting married or travelling. Without that, the guilt about leaving home would be even greater. Sometimes the weight of domestic responsibility can be huge, but there is the dilemma of knowing that while they may be needed at home, they also need to forge a separate identity.

Eliza, who has a brother with intellectual disabilities, talks of the guilt she feels.

> For a long time I always carried a sad torch for him, in the form of a constant inner sadness, not allowing myself to enjoy real happiness without always being sure to remind myself of his misfortune. Finally I accepted that my guilt does not make him feel any better. And when I hold myself back from fully feeling joy, he neither knows about it or benefits from it. This sounds obvious, but ideas forged as children are difficult to dismiss.
>
> My guilt makes me feel responsible for him, and yet makes me want to run away – because, according to my inner child's reasoning, no amount of sacrifice could ever be enough. And at any time that I may say I don't have or want to give any more time or energy . . . well, then I'm the bad person again.

Julie, whose sister has some intellectual disabilities, says:

> I feel guilty that I don't spend more time with her. Guilt is a big thing. I have my life with four normal kids. She comes to dinner once a fortnight. She has lived in different housing situations – some not very nice – and when I would drop her

off I'd feel very guilty. I just hope she doesn't feel too envious of my family and children. She goes off alone to her flat.

Many siblings go on to develop very successful lives, through high academic and sporting achievements. However, it can be a two-edged sword. At a young age, these children can also feel guilty when they do achieve success if, at the same time, they see their brother or sister struggling over the most basic of activities. As Rachel said, she still needs to convince herself that it is okay to be okay. There can be constant dissonance between needing to be perfect, but feeling guilty when success follows.

If a brother or sister is sent to an institution, it is easy for a young sibling to believe they might be to blame for their parents' decision. The guilt can stay with them forever, even if explanations are given at a later stage. For other siblings, the immense relief about the child's departure may cause guilt.

Some siblings adopt certain behaviour in an attempt to appease their guilt. Helping out with a brother or sister with special needs can be positive in that a child can feel he is contributing to the family. Such activities can contribute to the development of healthy self-esteem. However, overdoing the caring in an effort to deal with guilt can be unhealthy. Siblings can become used to always putting the needs of another before their own. This can be particularly unhealthy if the child has also adopted the role of 'people pleaser'. Such roles can continue into adulthood, and be played out in relationships, inhibiting equality and growth. Siblings might become compulsive helpers, not knowing other ways to act. They might define themselves as carers and not know when to stop. They may never have learnt how to look after their own needs. Sometimes this leads to burnout. Alternatively, the responsibility can be too onerous, causing siblings to distance themselves from the family as they move into adulthood. This can also add to guilt and isolation.

Summary

- Siblings may have a range of feelings that are difficult to discuss, including anger, depression, embarrassment, fear and guilt.
- Not talking about the feelings just makes them worse – the most important gift we can give children is the ability to talk about how they feel.

- When children feel they cannot express certain feelings, the distress might show up in their behaviour. For example, withdrawal, acting-up, anxiety, stomach-aches, becoming a 'people-pleaser' or the 'good' child.

Key strategies to deal with these issues

- Communication about feelings – see pages 154–162.
- Help children find appropriate ways to deal with the feelings – see pages 160–162.
- Prepare children for others' reactions – see pages 168–170.
- Encourage independence – see pages 165–167.
- Sibling groups – see pages 172–177.

6

Ongoing grief

At what point do I get to cry over it? The answer has been, never. – *Tara*

As a society we have difficulty discussing disability in terms of grief; we are trying to promote disability as a 'difference' rather than anything that should bring about grieving. The reality for many families, however, is that a child's disability is a huge disappointment and until the sense of loss can be acknowledged and expressed, it is difficult to move on.

All members of a family in which there is disability experience loss: the person with the disability, parents, other children and extended family. Grief is often unrecognised, but in fact it is a chronic sorrow that continues throughout a lifetime. Many families are able to pick up the pieces and find new meaning in changed directions. They can still love and laugh, but there may be lasting heartache that keeps surfacing, often at times when it's least expected.

In order to understand the grief of siblings – which is less often recognised than that of other family members – it can be helpful to look first at the losses for parents.

Parents

For parents of a child with a disability, the losses can be far-reaching. At the same time, in the initial stages of diagnosing a child's disability, it is often unclear what the losses are for the child and what the future holds for him and his family. Parents suffer from the loss of dreams for their child's future, the loss of the 'normal' child they thought they would have, the loss of the family's future as they envisaged it. There can be loss of a sense of security or control over destiny and, in some cases, the loss of religious faith. Many, particularly women, lose their career, income and social networks. In some cases, bonding with the child may be affected. In other situations, a parent becomes so absorbed with the child (through love, protectiveness and sometimes guilt) that they shut themselves off from others around them, including their spouse and other children.

Parents' self-esteem can be severely shaken, which in turn affects their attitudes and coping strategies. They can be racked with guilt and have constant questions about what they could or should have done to prevent their child from suffering. One mother was afraid that the chemicals she had used cleaning the bathroom might have been the cause of her child's problems. Doctors told another mother that the probable cause of her child's disability was the influenza immunisation she had during pregnancy, even though she had been advised to have it by another doctor. She lived with that guilt for many years until genetic tests proved that the immunisation was not the cause.

Julie's mother carried guilt in another way.

> **My mother always felt responsible for my sister's illness; she felt she must have led a very bad life for this to happen to her.**

Some mothers may lose faith in their femininity, as defined by their ability to produce a healthy, active child. Fathers may have similar doubts about their masculinity and their ability to act as protector of their family.

Caroline tells of her anticipation leading up to her son's birth. He was born with heart problems and other disabilities. Instead of being surrounded by flowers and congratulatory cards, she was pretty much left alone. People didn't know how to respond and so they stayed away. She felt keenly the loss of all the large and small celebrations of her son's birth she had anticipated during her pregnancy, but received none of the sympathy and support she would have been given if her baby had died. She needed comfort and reassurance, but was told by her mother, 'Well, at least he isn't in a wheelchair,' as though that should be some consolation.

Often people don't know what to say and what comes out can be quite inappropriate. Joy finds it difficult when people say things like, 'But she looks so normal!' when referring to her daughter Sally, who has epilepsy and intellectual disabilities.

My sister-in-law commented once that it is sad about Sally, because she is so pretty. I think it is sad, even if she were ugly!

Various accepted psychological models that focus on the stages of grieving don't seem to fit the situation of families of people with disabilities. For example, it can be difficult to accept the reality of the loss. For parents of a child born with a disability, there are no rituals to help them come to terms with their loss and grief. They don't get to talk about it; some may be made to feel guilty if they even try to express their feelings. So their grief remains largely private and repressed. Holly Lu, the mother of a teenage son with multiple disabilities, talks about the difficulties of the grieving process.

When I think about the coping process, it seems to me that the Elizabeth Kubler-Ross [a psychiatrist who published *On Death and Dying* in the USA in 1969] model of the stages of grieving doesn't fit our experience of having a loved one with a disability. We don't move tidily through these well-defined stages, ending up in the magic place called 'acceptance'. Instead, we cycle through all those feelings – including several others, such as envy (of folks who don't seem to appreciate the gift of life without disability), frustration (with non-responsive, if not actively weapon-bearing service systems) – more like a ferris wheel than a straightforward climb up a ladder.

Parents of a child born with a disability may feel guilty about grieving too much or for too long. In some ways, it might seem like a negation of the child as he or she is. We are pressured by society and our best selves to love our children unconditionally. If parents grieve too much, they are saying, in effect, 'I don't love you one hundred per cent the way you are. I wish you were different.'

Grief is a process. If you don't work through the grief – understand, acknowledge and truly experience it – then it is hard to resolve the pain and loss. In the same way that people may experience a range of reactions to a death, parents of a child with a disability may go through shock and withdrawal, sadness, denial, despair, fear, anger and guilt. If these are not allowed an outlet, they might suffer subsequent physical or emotional problems.

One of the normal phases of grief, which Kubler-Ross discusses, is a feeling of anger, either at the person who died, or the world, or both. Again, some parents with a child with special needs can't allow themselves to feel anger at the child – that would be too unfair to contemplate when the child is so vulnerable. It's easy for the anger to be turned inward and build on existing guilt or anxiety. If anger is left unexpressed, it is difficult to resolve the grief and, in some cases, can result in parental depression, substance abuse, or even abuses of their child with special needs or their other children. For some, the 'system' becomes the focus of their anger. Although in many cases this might be quite understandable and reasonable, for some parents the aggression toward the system can become unhealthy for themselves and their child.

For parents of a child with a disability, grief resurfaces throughout their lifetime as they are reminded of their own and their child's loss, especially when their other children or friends' children reach different milestones. Many may feel that they have come to terms with the situation, but then will be reminded again of what could have been. It can be difficult finding resolution given the unending tasks they face and the unfixable nature of their child's disability. Caroline reflects on the pain.

> **I don't feel we ever can complete the grief process. The pain and loss will always be there; it is a day-by-day roller-coaster ride of emotions. When do we start to grieve and when do we end?**

Joy's daughter Sally started at a 'normal' kindergarten but then transferred to a special school for children with disabilities. Many of the children from her kindergarten had gone on to the school which her older daughter, Rose, attended.

> **We went to Rose's end-of-year concert at school. I was sitting there, watching the children perform, with my husband and new baby. I recognised some of the children from Sally's kindergarten class and suddenly realised that if things had been different for Sally, I would have been watching her sing with the class on stage. This was the class that Sally should have been in. The feelings of overwhelming grief swept over me, once again.**

Having a third child, Catrina, has triggered new emotions in Joy. She revisits the feelings she had when waiting for Sally's diagnosis and feels enormous sadness when she remembers the difficulties of the early years and how hardly any mothers spoke to her at Sally's kindergarten. She feels sad that Sally has no little friends and can't do ballet and other activities like her sister. She realises they will have to teach Catrina about Sally's disabilities, and that Catrina's development will overtake Sally's in a few years.

My parents had difficulty acknowledging and coming to terms with their own grief. Mum and Dad had come from a generation that didn't talk readily about feelings; you just got on and did what you had to do. My mother told me that for weeks after hearing of my sister's diagnosis, she walked the streets of the town where they lived, pushing her baby's pram and crying. She would go home and clean herself up each night, ready for when my father returned from work. One day she just said to herself, 'This has to stop, I need to handle this and get on with life.' She no longer walked and cried.

My father went off to work each day. He had no outlet for his own pain. If his child had died he would have been given compassionate leave, time off for grieving. But in this situation, he too had to just get on with the job. I don't believe he ever cried. He submerged himself in his work and now wonders about the effect of that on my mother. There was certainly no counselling or other support to help them deal with their emotions.

Within a marriage there can be differences in how each partner deals with their grief. In general, women find it easier to express their feelings about loss. Men often feel they need to be strong, to be in control, not to show emotion and to be there for others. They are expected not to cry or show vulnerability. Often men need more time before they are ready to discuss the implications of the disability.

Joy tells of the frustration in trying to get her husband to talk.

> **Sally had had a long seizure during a family holiday. As a result she was taken by helicopter back to the city hospital. We had to pack up the holiday house and drive back to the hospital, not knowing what we were going back to. Sally ended up being okay, but when we returned home, all I wanted to do was sit down and talk about what had happened, be hugged and have a good cry.**
>
> **I wanted to know that *we* would be okay and that we could face together whatever life was presenting us with. All James wanted to do was be by himself, to think. So he went**

> **outside and mowed the lawns. I can remember sitting on a seat on our porch crying and feeling more alone than I had ever felt before. I kept thinking, 'My baby has something terribly wrong with her and how will we cope with all this if James can't even give me a hug and talk about it?'**
>
> **On reflection, I can now see we were both feeling overwhelmed by the situation and were each dealing with it in our own way. Later, we did talk about things and our relationship has been strengthened by it all. I had to accept, though, that we were going to have to go on our own journeys to survive it together in the end.**

Josie tells a similar story about her father.

> **My mum now jokes about it but my brother was born at the beginning of summer. Every morning my dad exercised – ran, biked and lifted weights. Every night after my brother and I were in bed he would go outside and sit and stare at the sky. My mother said that she wanted to talk about how their new baby was going to affect their lives and my dad just wanted to be alone. She experienced a loneliness like no other. She says that it really upset her that he didn't want to talk about it, but she says that something just kept telling her to leave him alone out there at night, staring.**
>
> **After some time, my dad was ready to talk about what had happened during the previous months. My mum now says she is sure that if she had pressured him early on they never would have made it through. She realises it was his way of coming to terms with the life he had expected versus the life he was given. It was my dad's way of accepting what was going to happen during the next 50-plus years of his life and accepting the loss of the son he thought he was going to have.**
>
> **He has always been a wonderful father to both my brother and me – very involved and very loving – but I definitely think mums and dads handle the birth of a child with disabilities very differently and there may be a lot less marriages in trouble if there was someone there to help the parents work through their feelings.**

These parents could have been helped enormously if early support had provided an understanding of each other's different needs. Joy observes that she has seen several marriages break down because of the stress in the early years of dealing with a child with a disability.

On the other hand, while the stress and grief can contribute to trouble in a marriage, a couple's relationship may be strengthened by all that they have gone through together. This obviously depends on how healthy the relationship was before the child's disability. Supporting each other through pain, disappointment and celebrations can create an unbreakable bond that sustains partners through a lifetime. Each parent needs reassurance of the other's commitment. Again, early support from outside the marriage can be of enormous benefit in the long term.

Siblings

It can be even more difficult for siblings to understand and express their losses than it is for their parents. Children with a brother or sister with a disability have to grow up quickly, and be responsible. In the process, they lose some of their childhood.

Siblings who are older than the child with a disability have a period of 'normal' family life when they can share all the usual activities with parents and possibly other siblings. Along with the rest of the family they anticipate the approaching birth of a baby with excitement and imagined scenarios. But that can all come unstuck when a child is born with a disability. Siblings know there is something wrong, but well-meaning parents may shield them from the full picture as long as possible. Some parents, absorbed in their own distress, find it difficult to recognise or acknowledge the effects on siblings.

If siblings do start to understand the magnitude of the loss suffered by their brother or sister with a disability and the whole family, how can they possibly grieve for themselves? It feels too self-indulgent. What is their loss compared to that of their brother or sister, or that of their parents?

Nance says:

> **I don't know if I've ever really acknowledged my grief. I'm always so defensive if people feel sorry for me or pity me because of what we've been through. I always say how great Ashley is and how proud of his achievements I am and how I wouldn't be the same person without him. But at the same time, I just well up with tears when I think about him. It's like**

> **a double-edged sword. I feel his frustration, that he can't take control of his life as I can. I never bring up with Mum how he got sick when he was little, it still upsets her too much.**

Siblings who are younger than the child with a disability have even fewer opportunities to grieve. They are born into the role of sibling to a person with disabilities, and many don't really come to an understanding of their losses until adulthood. They may wonder what their brother or sister would be like if they didn't have disabilities, what their relationship would be like. When you are the only sibling, it is easy to wonder what it would be like to have a brother or sister with whom you could do the 'normal' things that other siblings do, and you have no one else in the family who can relate to your feelings. As Josie explains:

> **As the only other sibling, we have had no one to share our heartaches with. Our parents had each other and they understood each other's feelings ... but there has been no one in my life who has also had my brother as their brother ... and so at times I have felt sadness and not understood and I've noticed that those feelings get stronger as I get older.**
>
> **There are times when I would give anything in the world to know what it feels like to call my brother on the phone and talk.**

In my case, having my own family helped me to really understand my own loss. I saw my children sharing the full range of emotions – screaming with anger one minute, sitting with arms entwined the next. I began to feel the loss of a playmate, a confidante, a 'partner in crime', someone to share the birth of my children, someone to share the birth of hers, someone to share a past with, and someone to look forward to the future with. I still long for a 'normal' sister, more so as I get older.

Other siblings, also, have not recognised the need to grieve until later in life. Renee reflects on the difficulties.

> **I never spoke about it until I was an adult and then only to a very few trusted friends because I knew I would howl. I had never grieved. I had never done any of the things I needed to emotionally.**

Eliza talks of a range of issues.

> **I have often felt like grieving over my brother as though he had died because it feels like a death of all potential and**

> **possibility for who he could have been, individually and as a member of our family. But when do you start and when does it end? At what point do I get to cry over it? The answer has been never. As a sibling, from the time you understand the problem you are ushered into playing your supportive role in the family. No one has time or any extra energy to deal with the other sibling's grief. And I certainly did not want to burden my parents with any more needs.**

Caroline talks of her own father's grief. He had grown up with a sister with disabilities and then his grandson was born with disabilities.

> **It was only after becoming a grandfather of a disabled child that he talked about growing up with a disabled sister. For the first time in his life he truly grieved for the losses of childhood.**

Siblings go through different stages of grief over the losses associated with the disability. As they proceed through different educational levels, in some cases they might realise that their brother or sister will never be able to have the same experiences. Some grieve when they marry and wonder how it would have been if their sister could have been the bridesmaid. Each celebration, every rite of passage, can be a source of grief, knowing the other child will never experience the same fulfilment. Some hear others talk of their 'normal' sibs and the activities they enjoy together and the squabbles they have, and think, 'If only those people knew how lucky they are.' I remember being particularly jealous in my teens of one friend who had a brother and a sister. To me, it seemed like the ideal family and I fantasised about marrying the brother and becoming part of it.

Joy remembers her daughter Rose's sadness when she realised her sister Sally would not be going to the same school.

> **Rose had a number of children in her class with younger siblings starting school. We had hoped Sally was going to be able to go to the same school but it became obvious she needed a special school. Rose became very sad and teary when she saw her friends and their siblings playing together at school. In the end we arranged for Rose to go to Sally's school for a couple of visits, and her feelings began to resolve, for now.**

Losses can include memories of childhood. Many siblings don't have family holidays to remember. Meagan talks about her brother ruining her homework or damaging other possessions.

> **We had to get rid of trinkets and other things – he would destroy them all. I wish I had something left over from my childhood.**

Many siblings need counselling as adults to work through the grief and guilt. Most recognise the tremendous loss for their parents, but they also express the wish that parents and others would recognise their own losses. Eliza talks of the difficulty in focusing on her own future.

> **I think that siblings really grieve alone, or maybe never really get to grieve in a healthy way, which includes knowing when it's okay to stop grieving and focus on our future.**

Nance sums up the experience of many:

> **Talking about my brother and my relationship with him brings tears to my eyes, as it has so many other times in the past. And it is not because I feel particularly deprived, that in childhood I missed out on anything significant because of him. I'm the first to admit that there were difficult times, times of great sadness as well as the small victories that were celebrated out of proportion. It just seems there are many feelings there that I have never acknowledged and unfortunately, despite the great joy and pride I feel in his achievements now, speaking about him in an intimate, sharing way almost always brings out the tears.**

When a brother or sister with special needs dies, a sibling's feelings can be intensely complicated. They might feel a huge sense of loss over the life their sister or brother might have lived. Or they might feel relief, mixed with guilt for having that feeling. They may also experience guilt about not having done enough to contribute to the child's care.

Religion

Parents and siblings of someone with a disability may suffer yet another loss, a loss of faith. Religious faith can give strength in all sorts of adversity, but disability can sometimes provoke a turning away from long-held beliefs. Seeing your child suffer a chronic, terminal illness, or watching your brother struggle to walk or talk, or observing how your sister is dependent on others for the most basic functions can lead to a questioning of faith. For those whose faith has been shattered, it can be a major task to recreate a new sense of spirituality.

Some people explain the disability as 'God's will'. They say that it is 'for our own good', or that 'we were especially chosen by God to care for this special child'. This belief, if freely chosen by parents and siblings, can be of considerable comfort. Families can gain sustenance from the belief that their purpose in life is to care for the child with a disability. However, when religious figures or other family members or outsiders impose the belief on families of people with disabilities, it often has the opposite effect and adds more grief and suffering to their lives.

Some see a family member's disability as a punishment from God. One mother thought for years that her child with Down Syndrome had been her punishment for another child she had borne and given away when she was 16. A Catholic priest told another mother she had sinned and was to blame for her child's disability. It is hard for many people to accept the idea of a God who would give a child a disability as a response to the mother's transgressions. Another mother saw her son's disabilities as her absolution – caring for such a child would surely secure her a place in heaven.

Renee had her own crisis of faith in her late teens.

> **For me, a large thing happened when I was at university. At about age 18, I experienced an incredible crisis of faith when I studied philosophy. I had been brought up in a strict Catholic family. I was studying philosophy and the problem of evil. You start to question how it is that there can be a good and all-powerful God when there is such wretchedness in the world. This was brought home to me very pointedly, I think, because as a child I had gone through life being taught to pray, 'Thank you God for all the good that you've given me.' Well, what do you say to the God who has bestowed something awful on you? It was a real disturbance of my world view. I feel I worked through all that but, at 18, it was a crisis for me.**

We generally like to believe that the world makes sense and that there is a cause for everything. Young children often use this line of thought to blame themselves for any stress that may be occurring around them. Self-blame denies a child the chance to grieve. It also leads to a loss of self-esteem. Adults often have difficulty accepting that a child needs to grieve.

Telling a sibling, 'God chose you because He needed someone special to look after this little special child' can create all sorts of dilemmas in the mind of young children. They find it difficult to let themselves feel anger or sadness or any of the reasonable and natural feelings that may arise in living with someone with a disability, and may turn their anger on themselves instead.

I have spoken to many parents and siblings who found themselves unwelcome at church or openly ostracised because of a child's disability. In spite of being regular churchgoers during their early courtship and marriage, my own parents found no comfort there after my sister was born. They felt quite excluded. At a later stage, when they were back in the city, the same occurred. My sister obviously had a problem and no one tried to include her or my parents. My mother went back to church some time later but found the logistics of getting there difficult, as it meant leaving my father to deal with huge stresses at home. She talked to God in church one day, saying she could no longer leave her family at home in disarray on a Sunday morning. Certainly, the church did not reach out to my family.

For many people, however, church and a strong faith are important factors in their adjustment. A family can gain enormous social and emotional support through belonging to a church community.

Part of coping with a child with special needs involves creating more positive meanings out of the situation. With a strong faith it can sometimes be easier to create such meanings. But even without faith many families are still able to find inner strength and find positives in their situation. Some families say they have learnt the meaning of unconditional love, that the disability made the family much closer, and that they have learnt tolerance and compassion. This can take time, however, and depends very much on the support given by family, friends and professionals.

Summary

Parents

- The grief of disability is largely unrecognised and unsupported.
- It can be difficult talking to a partner about feelings.
- Your whole world view may be upset.

Siblings

- It is even more difficult to recognise and acknowledge the losses for children.
- Siblings can be helped to create more positive meanings out of their experiences.

Key strategies to deal with these issues

- Recognising the grief – see pages 130–131.
- Communication with your partner – see pages 128–130.
- Finding meaning – see page 131.
- Recognising the losses for children – see pages 170–171.
- Communication with siblings – see pages 150–160.
- Sibling groups – see pages 172–177.
- Social support – see pages 179–180.

7

Responsibility and caregiving

Growing up fast

> **I just wanted to be a kid and not have all those responsibilities.**
>
> *–Meagan*

Siblings of children with special needs are usually expected to grow up faster than their peers. While parents have to focus so much attention on the child with special needs, many siblings learn to look after themselves. In addition, they may be expected to put considerable time into caring for their brother or sister. If this is kept in balance there can be long-term benefits for the child, in terms of feeling valued and useful, and for the whole family. Too much responsibility, however, can interfere with normal social development and the establishment of independence. Some siblings feel the weight of the responsibility long before they are ready. They may become 'Mummy's little helper' or 'Daddy's right-hand man'. In sole-parent families this can become especially significant. Also, if a child with special needs makes no progress, a child who has been actively involved in the care may start to feel some responsibility for that.

Tara felt the ongoing pressures.

> **Adults always told me I was so mature for my age, so good to be spending time with my brother and helping my mother. I hated those comments so much. I just wanted to be a child.**

As an older and only able sibling I developed an extraordinary sense of responsibility for family and friends. I limit my friends as I can't cope with the 'obligation' I feel if the number of people close to me is too large.

I have learnt that as a child I internalised the need always to be okay, self-reliant and never need or accept help. It is a difficult lesson to un-learn and the repercussions as an adult – social and emotional isolation – are devastating.

A child's reactions may change over time. Nance started to feel differently as she approached her teens.

When I was very small, until perhaps eight or nine, I remember seeing myself as my brother's little protector, and being praised by every one of my parents' friends for being such a good girl looking after my brother. Then as I approached my teens, I remember feeling overwhelmed by what I then saw as a burden. I did not have a brother I could play cricket with, could confide in, or have what I saw as the 'normal' relationship all my friends had with their siblings.

It can be particularly difficult for siblings to develop true independence. Meagan was very aware that all her friends had more freedom. She felt isolated and different when she missed out on social activities with peers, but felt she couldn't complain.

I looked after my brother after school and in the holidays. All the other kids would talk about what they had done in the holidays, like go to movies. They could earn pocket money but I couldn't and they had the time and freedom to do things. I had friends at school but I felt alienated from them.

I'd say I needed help but Mum was too stressed and I didn't want to upset her, so I just dealt with it. Everyone says to me that they thought I was coping really well – but I wasn't. I just wanted to be a kid and not have all those responsibilities.

Many siblings look back and feel that they missed out on being young and having fun. The normal concerns of adolescence, such as fashion, music and the opposite sex, can seem trivial compared with the sometimes fragile life of a child with special needs. A sibling can feel out of tune with peers, which can lead to further isolation.

The child with special needs can be a direct barrier to social interaction. Fran, whose brother has Down Syndrome, just wanted to be able to share girl talk with her friend, but the responsibility for her brother was always there and interfered constantly with her social development.

> **When I went to see my friend up the road, I'd be told to take my brother with me. We would want to chat about boys and pop stars but I'd have to take him with me.**

Missi resented the time she needed to put in to her sister's care. As a result she was particularly eager to find some independence.

> **I always felt like I did a lot of my sister's caretaking when I got older. My parents wanted to be able to go out and be with each other, so they would leave me with her so that I could feed her and take care of her until bedtime. I think I just always felt like her mother. I had to make so many sacrifices for my family. I had to quit activities I enjoyed so much so they would be happy – and I hated it! I couldn't wait to leave home. I still have the same problem of being the caregiver for all my friends and not taking it from them in return.**

Lily, nine, talks of her caring role with her older brother with autism.

> **He's always awake at night. Sometimes he comes into my room and wants to play; he jumps on my bed. I wake up and try to scream at him quietly so he doesn't wake up Mummy. And then I take him back to bed and tuck him in and tell him to shut up and not wake up again. Sometimes I feel bad when I yell at him.**

Tim, 16, adds:

> **We are lucky as a family to have my brother in respite four nights a week so we can function more normally then. When he is here he needs constant supervision. I am in my final year of school and the nights when my brother is around I can't do any schoolwork – everything needs to be focused on him. It can be tiring and frustrating. Wherever we go I constantly have to watch and worry about what he is doing.**

There has been a move in recent years to 'mainstream' children with disabilities into so-called normal schools. In many respects this makes sense, not only for the child with a disability but for society as a whole. However, there needs to be some thought given to the effect on brothers or sisters. Susan talks of the need to protect her sister, who has Down Syndrome, while they were going to the same school, and her feelings when that changed.

> I started at the same school as my sister. I always fought her fights in the playground. It was such a relief to me when my parents moved her to a special school and I felt free. I feel guilty saying that but it was like a weight being lifted off my shoulders.

When a sibling is the younger child

Younger children may find it even more difficult caring for a brother or sister who is older and bigger. Normally older children will care for younger ones in this situation, but for younger siblings the situation is different. They may experience guilt for being more competent than their older sibling and this can lead to ambivalence about surpassing the child with special needs.

Gina was younger than her sister who is deaf.

> Though chronologically my sister was older, in terms of responsibility I was the oldest because she couldn't communicate verbally. We were very much on a par in terms of maturity.
>
> We communicated very well because I was her voice. She and I signed. Very few of the rest of the family signed, so I was her link with everyone else in the family. This was a big responsibility for me. Everyone said, 'Gina is such a *good* child.' I was always the good one. This was the expectation of me and this is what I tried to be. There was embarrassment but there was real responsibility.
>
> My parents' expectation was that I would be good, be helpful. I would be the one who would be my sister's parent if they were not there. I was the parent and yet I was younger. And yet I was reminded constantly that I was 'just the kid'. She was older and she would take precedence in so many instances and yet I knew that I was the one who had the hard slog, who was the responsible one. I had to look after her and yet she took precedence.
>
> People would say something to her – she was taller than me – and she would look at them and then at me and I would

say, 'She's deaf, I'll tell you what she wants.'

From a very young age I would do that and people would be quite impressed. They would say, 'Look at this little kid, she's looking after her sister.' And I would think, 'Yeah, I am too!' But it was difficult. I tried to think positively or I would have been very angry.

Finding the positives

> **My brother has been the most influential person in my life and continues to be each day . . . all I have to do is think about him and I am able to smile.** *–Josie*

Providing care for a brother or sister can bring many positives. If their own needs are met, if they believe that they are special too and that their feelings are important, siblings have much to gain by being actively involved with a brother or sister with special needs. If the care-giving is kept in balance and is valued by the family – rather than taken for granted – caring for a brother or sister can add to a sibling's self-esteem and sense of accomplishment. Families may become closer as they share the challenges and celebrate the successes of the family together. Siblings may feel tremendous pride in the achievements of their brother or sister. They can gain enormous satisfaction from being involved in helping their brother or sister, or teaching them new skills.

If not overdone, such responsibility can lead to an improvement in how the children interact and play together. There may be a bonding that would not occur without the care-giving. Josie talks of bonding with her younger brother.

> **I truly think that taking care of my brother helped me better understand my parents and my brother. And I connected with him and bonded with him in a way that I never would have, had I not had the responsibility of watching him. Now I am the only person that he lets hang all over him and hug him for long amounts of time. We take car rides and only with me does he sit up front. With my parents he sits in the back because he grabs the steering wheel or gear shift but with me he just sits in the seat and smiles and rocks back and forth to the loud music that my parents probably don't play.**

As well as caregiving, many siblings attribute their positive feelings to the attitudes of their parents. Josie says her parents understood that she needed some privacy and needed to express all her feelings. She adds:

> **I would say my favourite thing in the world that my brother has given me is a true understanding of the words 'unconditional love'. He has also taught me to be compassionate, less judgemental, an advocate for him and others. And he has taught me to appreciate the small things in life.**

At 24, Mark has two older brothers, Sam, who is able, and Dean, who has cerebral palsy. Mark, also, believes his positive attitude towards his brother largely stems from his mother and father.

> **We three boys were always treated equally. Dean did get a little more attention but we understood that. Dean was always included in all family outings and he always got along with everyone. Mum and Dad let us live our lives as 'normal' as possible. Sam and I played tennis from a very early age and went through all the different stages of Scouts, basically did all the things we wanted to do even though we had a disabled brother. I still went out with friends and did all the teenage things. It made us realise that if we all worked together we could still do everything.**
>
> **I don't feel embarrassed. Instead, I feel proud of him. Maybe I see things differently because I have a disabled brother, but often I sit back and think how lucky I am. For several years I helped out with Dean's disabled Scout group and enjoyed every bit of it. I also like to help Mum and Dad with looking after Dean. Recently I looked after him for a weekend so they could have a short holiday.**
>
> **I will always be a big part of Dean's life and wouldn't change a thing as it has made me a much better person.**

Some parents, in good faith, avoid giving their other children any extra caregiving role. This can deprive them of opportunities to feel useful. The key is to achieve a balance between a child feeling they have an important role to play and being overburdened with responsibility. Many siblings find enormous inspiration through watching their brother or sister's struggles and achievements. One famous example is athlete Cathy Freeman, whose older sister was born with cerebral palsy. Other factors obviously played a role in her enormous athletic success. As a child, however, when asked why she liked athletics, Cathy would reply: 'I have a sister, Anne Marie, who has cerebral palsy, and my mother told me that I had two good arms and two good legs, so use them.' (*Australian*, 26 September 2000)

Siblings of people with disabilities often grow up to be more compassionate, caring and tolerant of differences. They often have maturity beyond their years and an outlook on life that makes them acutely aware of their blessings. They recognise which are the important issues and which are not. Together with the pride they may feel, they often have protective feelings toward their brother or sister with special needs. Josie says:

> **I love my brother like I love no other, a protective and concerned love. I'm usually such a laidback person but if anyone tried to hurt my brother I would be a totally different kind of person. There's a passion about him that is unexplainable and truly brings out this other side of me – an overprotective, overbearing, angry big sister.**

This can carry over to a broader consciousness of others' needs and many siblings go on to be advocates, not only for their brother or sister, but for people with disabilities in general. Some people with disabilities are unable to speak for themselves and siblings are often in a good position to take on that role.

Missi feels she can be a more supportive friend through her experiences as a sibling.

> **I do think that it has made me more compassionate and understanding. I have always been the one that my friends come to when they need to talk or they need a shoulder to cry on, so that is a good thing that has come of this.**

Siblings tend to be more conscious of others' feelings. They talk of being supersensitive to jokes about disability and jibes about 'retards' and the like. Often, they are careful not to make fun of others, knowing too well how that feels. Tim adds:

> **My brother's special needs make me reflect quite a lot on what kind of person I would be if he wasn't around, especially when kids use terms like 'spastic' to put people down. I wonder if I would be like them and not know anything about the problems faced by families in this situation.**

This can follow through to other generations. For my own children, having an auntie with special needs adds a dimension to their lives that is hard to measure. They, too, seem more sensitive to the feelings of others, especially those who are picked on or who are less fortunate than themselves.

Summary

- Siblings can feel the burden of responsibility at a young age.
- If the responsibility is not too great, a sibling can gain a sense of competence through contributing to the care of a brother or sister with special needs.
- A sibling needs to be able to develop his own life separate from the family.
- If supported, siblings can develop a range of positive qualities such as strength, tolerance, compassion, a sense of responsibility, insight, maturity, pride and the ability to achieve.

Key strategies to deal with these issues

- Value the care given by a sibling – see pages 164–165.
- Encourage siblings to develop their independence – see pages 165–167.

8

The future

How do I know how much I am supposed to give? I really wish I knew. –*Eliza*

As siblings move into adulthood, new issues emerge. They might ask questions like: What will happen when my parents die? Will I need to care for my brother or sister in my own home? Will they live in a group home? Who will manage their finances and medical needs? Will they be able to be employed? Will I find a future spouse who will accept my brother or sister? Do I want children of my own? How will I cope if one of them has special needs?

Life choices

Regardless of a sibling's emotional well-being, there are issues that affect all siblings and their choices about the future. Josie, in her early twenties, sums up the concerns of many siblings.

> **I guess that someone from a 'normal' (whatever that is!) family would be thinking of their future: Where are they going? Where do they want to be in five, 10, 15 years? Are they going to have children? How many do they want? Will they get married? Where do they want to live? Far from their parents, near their parents? And the list goes on. And then take sibs like us and on top of all those questions we are also thinking: Where do I want to live *and* how can I make sure I make the right decision regarding my brother or sister? Do I want kids? What if they have a disability? Can I handle that along with taking care of my brother or sister? If I move away from my parents, am I a bad sib because not only am I leaving them, I**

am leaving my brother or sister? Not only am I thinking of my own future, but I am also worried about and planning for my brother's future.

With all the issues involved it can be difficult for siblings to make life choices. In addition, they often feel pressure to consider their parents. Sometimes that extends to not making decisions without parental approval. Siblings can grow up lacking confidence about making decisions or going against their parents' beliefs or wishes.

Even though parents may encourage their children to make decisions themselves, often a sibling will continue to be influenced by their childhood. As Nance says:

I can't help myself. I am always conscious of trying to be the best I can, not only for myself but for the family as well. When you are the sibling of someone with a disability you basically just can't help taking everyone else into account, rightly or wrongly, when you are making decisions. Because it's something you've just had to grow up with. It's a hard habit to break.

I don't know if other 'normal' siblings are affected so strongly by their brother or sister, but I know I can look back on the major decisions of my life and know that my brother is a major factor in almost every one.

Choosing a career

Many siblings of people with disabilities enter the caring professions. They have been influenced by their experiences in ways that develop their sense of social justice and social equity, resulting in a desire to support disadvantaged groups within the community. They generally understand and appreciate the differences between people, are able to show empathy and compassion, and are drawn to special education, occupational therapy, social work and similar vocations. Siblings also learn a variety of caregiving skills in early life and it seems natural to put these to use in a helping profession. A myriad of factors influence career choice, of course, but for siblings the overriding one is often their family situation.

Tara says:

I am a social worker. I was always going to be a social worker, watching out for others, providing a compassionate ear,

> **problem-solving difficult situations. I love my job and my childhood experiences have certainly helped me in the role.**

Rachel was drawn to working with people with disabilities.

> **I became an occupational therapist because of my sisters and growing up with them, and I love my profession.**

Some siblings might go into the helping professions in an effort to appease their guilt, which is not unhealthy if siblings are able to consider their own needs as well. Carly acknowledges this influence on her own decision.

> **As an adult, I have a career, which I began at the age of 18, working with people with disabilities. I think part of this career choice was due to guilt over my feelings and thoughts toward my brother; but I enjoy what I do and am successful at it.**

Others suggest siblings have spent much of their time having contact with service providers while growing up and so feel comfortable in that environment. It seems likely, however, that the majority of siblings who move into such service careers do so because they have acquired a sense of social justice as well as a range of appropriate skills.

Where to live

Siblings can feel torn between being supportive of their family and creating their own life. Many assume that they will care for their brother or sister in their own home and so find it hard to think about moving to an area distant from the family. Even if a brother or sister is in supported accommodation, these siblings experience a lifelong sense of responsibility to provide company or other supports to all the family.

Sometimes this comes easily, other times there can be confusion about choices. Opportunities that arise further from home can leave siblings grappling with feelings of guilt, and a fear that they are being selfish. They might feel conflicting loyalties to friends/spouses and their original family, and resentment that others can fly the coop without these same pressures.

Nance talks about her decision to move away to another state as part of her career development.

> **Making the decision to move was agonised over, at least partly because it meant I would not be able to keep up my weekly or bi-weekly visit routine to my brother. It seems silly to have to take that into account when planning your career, but I knew the impact it would have, not only on him, but on Mum and Dad, and that they would have to take on a greater burden of time with him. I know I have to make decisions for myself but I can't help feeling the guilt of leaving. Every time I go home for holidays I spend about a third of the time either seeing my brother or trying to arrange volunteers to spend time with him, to take up at least part of the role I feel I have abandoned.**
>
> **I know other 'normal' brothers and sisters never need to make those kind of decisions – in fact it is fine if they go for months without seeing each other – but it is not clear cut in my case and I do feel guilty.**

One sibling, in her early twenties, had moved to another state for a year. She told me it was wonderful to get away from the family for a while, but she added that expressing that thought brought enormous guilt.

Relationships

Many siblings are conscious that they need to choose a partner in life who can accept a brother or sister with special needs. Nance says:

> **I realise I have to be extremely careful who I choose for a lifelong partner – that they are fully aware of my brother, respectful of him, and get on well with him. Not only that, they need to be aware that at some stage, when my parents are no longer here, a degree of responsibility is going to fall on me. These, I realise, are added impediments to the already difficult task of finding the person you want to spend the rest of your life with. But then, I sometimes think that in a strange way, I'm actually lucky to have my brother to help me choose the right person. I wouldn't want to live with someone who couldn't get on with my brother and didn't understand his needs. To me it would show them up to be a selfish kind of person I wouldn't want to be with anyway.**

Siblings talk of judging not only dates, but friends too, on the basis of how they relate to their brother or sister. Nance continues:

> **All my life I have used my brother as a bit of a litmus test for my friends. The ones who passed into the realm of close friends were always the ones who accepted him well. I realise this was sometimes cruel, especially for people who have never met an intellectually disabled person before, and were naturally wary. But the people I really wanted to get to know were those who treated my brother with respect and didn't talk down to him.**

Others feel fearful about taking friends home, often waiting until they know someone well before disclosing information about their family situation. This can stem back to fears of being judged badly themselves or even being rejected completely.

Having children

Decisions about having children can be fraught with difficulty for siblings. Some feel they will be better equipped to handle any difficult situation, even if they were to have a child with a disability themselves. Others are terrified of the prospect. I was 35 when I became pregnant with my first child and was full of fear about what might be. Because of that fear and my age, my husband and I decided to have an amniocentesis, where a sample of amniotic fluid is tested for abnormalities. It provided no real guarantees, as it eliminated only certain problems, and besides, my sister's disability was not genetically based. However, we certainly felt some reassurance when the test ruled out major genetic problems.

Where a disability is genetically based, siblings can now seek genetic counselling as a way of assessing their own risks. Again, though providing no guarantees, this can be a helpful step in making the decision about having children. A general practitioner can refer you to the nearest genetic counselling service.

Marsha, whose sister has cerebral palsy and intellectual disabilities, took quite some time to feel comfortable about starting a family.

> **Whenever I saw kids or thought of having one, I just cried and cried. The fear of a disabled child was too much to handle. I went into counselling, came to terms with my grief over my sister and was able to overcome the fear and had two wonderful boys.**

Rachel had similar difficulties

> **Having kids must be one of the biggest issues for us sibs. From 16 years of age I started telling myself, 'I don't want kids, I don't want kids,' because I knew that when I was older I might think I really did want them. I was essentially trying to brainwash myself at a young age. After meeting my husband and knowing he wanted a child, it took me about eight years of counselling and self-discovery before I was ready.**

Most people are aware of the chances of 'something going wrong' but siblings have a more acute realisation of the risks. They know something went wrong before and it is easy to believe it will again. Some choose not to have their own children because their fears are too great.

Tara says:

> **The question of children or not is so big for me that I totally avoid the kinds of relationships where the issue may arise.**

Victoria felt that her own problems would have made mothering difficult.

> **While I would have loved to have children, I realise how many psychological issues I've had to deal with, and I am glad I did not burden any children with my emotional scars.**

Some siblings don't want to take on the responsibility of their own child because they know that they will ultimately have responsibility for a brother or sister. Others find that after years of feeling neglect and finally feeling that their life is their own, they don't want to give up that freedom.

It is clear there are a range of concerns for siblings as they look toward the future. For many it can feel a heavy burden. And it is easy to feel that no one understands. As Josie says:

> **No one really tries to understand what it has felt like to be me. They acknowledge that my parents have a lot to think about regarding the future – but I never hear support about what *my* future will be like when my mum and dad are older. I'm the only 'normal' child and I have a younger brother who is 22 but functions at the level of a one-year-old. It would be nice to hear someone say, 'Josie, how are you**

dealing with things? How has your brother affected you?' No one asks that because they assume he has affected me in only positive ways.

He's made me caring, non-judgemental, responsible, mature, aware of societal injustices and empathic. Everyone sees those qualities because they are easy to see, but not many people take the time to look at me and also see the not-so-good traits, like my 'good daughter' complex, my insane expectations of myself, my insecurities about the future, my worries about having my own children one day, about how my brother will affect my own family one day, about what happens when my parents need assistance with their daily living – along with my brother – and me being the only other sibling!

My brother's keeper

> **I am the designated person to care for my sisters after my parents are gone! Gasp . . . I am the only one! My mum has extended family I can at least use for support. So I better start talking to them about all this stuff!** – *Rachel*

Most siblings are acutely aware that they will need to take over when their parents are no longer able. For some, that involves caring for a brother or sister in their own home. Where a brother or sister lives in supported accommodation, siblings are often active in providing other support. They may provide social contact, management of finances, and medical care. Siblings often need help to understand issues such as guardianship, as a legal guardian may be required to make decisions for their brother or sister. (See chapter 10.)

Some siblings say they have used marriage, travel or other commitments as an escape from the pressures they feel as they reach adulthood. The burden can be even greater for siblings who have no able brothers or sisters. They may need to distance themselves for a short period in order to gain some independence. Often, they are then ready to face their increased responsibilities.

Other siblings, however, stay away for good. During the writing of this book, at dinner one night I met a man who has a sister with Down Syndrome. He admitted he has totally distanced himself from his family as he finds the whole situation too difficult. He initially agreed to an interview with me but it became clear that he preferred to avoid thinking about it as it caused him distress. When family members move away like this, other able siblings can be left with the full responsibility, leading to resentment and eventual family breakdown.

Tara struggled for some time with her attempts at independence.

> **I was 24 when I finally left my family. I had moved out some time before but remained a daily caregiver. I had to move to another state to escape and collapse in private. I felt so guilty I had run that I called every day and flew home every couple of months for three years. I am in so much financial debt and am still exhausted.**

Missi has a number of fears for the future.

> **I am the only other child in the family so that's kind of a pain. I've always wondered if things would be different if I had someone to talk to about the situation. I sometimes wonder what will happen when my parents die. What will happen to my sister? She's always lived with us at home and it would be so hard to let her live in a group home but equally hard on me to be her carer, knowing how much work she is.**

Julie tends to put off thinking about the future and what it holds.

> **When it comes to my responsibility when my parents aren't here, I think I have an 'ostrich' attitude. I won't think about it until it is necessary. Our mother's anxiety about different problems concerning our sister pulls me and my two brothers together. We talk about it and so we share it, but we're all hiding it under the carpet at the moment. We're all busy. I know that being the female, when the time comes, it will be me who does more of the everyday things. I'll need to clean her house and she will need more help as her mental faculties diminish even further, as they inevitably will with age.**

Eliza also grapples with how much she should give of herself.

> **I work hard to believe that my life is my own and not feel guilty that I have my own time, money and pleasures, even though my mentally retarded brother cannot have them. How**

do I know how much I am supposed to give? I really wish I knew.

Josie, whose brother has multiple disabilities and requires considerable day-to-day care, talks of a conflict of loyalty.

There is one part of me that feels like no one would take care of him with the kind of love and patience that I would, and then there is a part of me that feels like I also need to take care of myself and my future family, and I just don't know if a husband, children and brother all in my home would be too much for me to handle. I go back and forth on this issue, never sure how to feel or what to do . . . always happy that I haven't had to make the decision yet. My parents had over 30 years of their lives without the responsibility of him and I just have to remind myself that I have a right to that freedom too. But the guilt gets me. If I decide that I cannot take care of him every day for the rest of my life, am I a terrible, selfish sister? I do know that whatever happens I will always make sure that my brother and I live a very short distance from each other.

Siblings are more likely to remain involved in the life of a brother or sister with special needs if they have received support themselves. It also helps if there has been some preparation for the future. Providing support and planning for the future are discussed more fully in the next section of the book.

Summary

Siblings face a range of life choices as they move into adulthood. These include such questions as:

- Should I live near or far from my parents and brother or sister with special needs?
- Will I use the skills learnt in childhood in my chosen career?
- Will I find a mate who will be prepared to share the responsibility?
- Should I have my own children?
- How high are my risks of having a child with special needs?
- How much care should I give to my brother or sister?

Key strategies to deal with these issues

- Thinking about life choices – see pages 114–116.
- Planning for the future – see pages 142–145.

strategies

Introduction

The shared stories of siblings raise a multitude of issues for families and health practitioners. In the next section I describe a range of strategies, for adult siblings, parents and service providers, which may help to counter any negative impact that growing up with a disabled child in the family can have on siblings.

Adult siblings will discover ways to accept the role their sibling has played in making them who they are. Parents and service providers who are involved with families with young siblings will discover ideas for providing support and preventing problems arising.

Chapter 9 explores how adult siblings can gain understanding, discover needs, learn to express feelings and gain support, both from within and outside the family. The process involves making sense of the past and looking more confidently toward the future. Through exploring the difficult parts of your story, it might be possible to highlight some of the good things gained through your experiences.

Younger siblings are especially reliant on parents and service providers. Chapter 10 offers strategies for parents to build stronger families and chapter 11 includes specific strategies for supporting young siblings. Through focusing on building stronger families we can ensure siblings develop into stronger children and adults. A strong family can help a child adjust more positively to his or her situation.

Service providers are also able to help siblings through direct intervention and by assisting parents to learn ways to support all their children. Chapter 12 offers strategies for practitioners and advises parents how effective practitioners can help the family.

9

Adult siblings

Making sense of the past and moving forward

If you are a sibling, it is likely you have had a range of reactions after reading of others' experiences. You may have felt huge relief to realise others feel the same way as you do. On the other hand, you may not have related much at all to the stories here. Your story may be a more positive one; you may feel at ease with the influence your brother or sister has had on your life; you may be more comfortable with the future.

It is important to remember we each have different responses to being a sibling of someone with special needs, and *all* these responses are valid. For those who have experienced difficulties it might be helpful just to know that you are not alone in your experiences, and that there are steps you can take to help deal with your concerns.

I have learnt that the most important way to heal and grow is to understand the feelings we experience and be able to express them in an environment of validation and support. To gain strength it is important to understand how you have been influenced by your childhood experiences, and what your needs are now. How have your feelings affected your behaviour? What are the implications for your family and other relationships now? How might these relationships be affected in the future?

You need to use the information in this book in your own way and time. Of course, if your experience was largely positive, you may not need to go through all the steps suggested here.

Reading through them, however, may still give you an opportunity to grow.

Gain understanding

Think about how your feelings as a child may have been reflected in how you behaved or thought about things, and whether you are still following similar patterns in your life. Did you act out your feelings in disruptive behaviour, or did you withdraw? Have you become a 'people pleaser', or do you strive for perfection? Do you feel overly responsible for everything and everyone? Do you feel guilty about the happiness in your life and as a result have you developed self-harming or self-defeating behaviour? Do you feel guilty if you start to think of the not-so-good aspects of your childhood?

As you think through these questions, don't be surprised if defensive reactions sometimes build up that prevent you from recognising the pain of childhood. It can be difficult to acknowledge the effects of our experiences as it feels like we're blaming parents and others. This just adds to the guilt. The process can be a slow and painful one, as Tara explains.

> **As a professional in child health, I was drawn to siblings and I facilitated the development of several support programs. After about six months I picked up a book written by a sibling and literally fell apart. It took this powerful story to allow me to recognise my own childhood and to understand my fears, my passion, my grief. It was the start of a very powerful and pain-laden recovery.**

Like Tara, the first book I read on sibling issues touched me in indescribable ways. It resonated with something hidden within me and, with every word, the burden I had carried for all those years seemed gradually to lighten. I couldn't get enough. As well as gaining understanding, the knowledge that others had similar experiences created enormous relief. To discover that this is a genuine field of study was an incredible source of validation for me.

I wrote earlier that some siblings have found a close relationship to be a catalyst for looking at some of these issues. One sibling had difficulty expressing anger with her husband and realised, through therapy, that this was largely due to her

Being a sibling

In order to improve your understanding you might like to think about the following aspects of your childhood. They might act as cues for you to write about your experiences, and they might help you to become more aware of what you are feeling, and why.

How did you find out about your brother or sister's special needs?
What were the effects of the special needs on your family relationships?
What were the effects on your parents' marriage?
Were they were supportive of each other?
Did your parents seem depressed or angry?
What are your feelings about the disability, your brother or sister and yourself: the good things and the not-so-good things?
How do you feel if you think or write about your negative reactions/feelings?
How do you feel about the responsibilities assigned to you?
Were you acknowledged for the help you gave?
Did you try to be the 'good' child or try in other ways to be perfect/successful?
Did you withdraw or misbehave when things were difficult?
What was your experience of school?
Was there open communication in your family?
If you couldn't talk of feelings in your family, were there others with whom you could talk?
What messages did you receive from parents and others about how you should behave/feel?
Did you have opportunities for privacy?
What fears did you have for your brother or sister, such as concerns for their survival?
Did you have fears about them hurting you or damaging your things?
Did you have any other fears?

Did you feel your parents 'spoiled' your brother or sister with special needs?
How fair did you feel things were in your family?
Has guilt played a part in your life?
What have been the effects on your education and other recreational activities?
What have been the effects on your social life and relationships?
Were you embarrassed?
How did you respond to teasing directed at your brother or sister or at you about them?
Have you been included in plans made for your sibling, such as respite, accommodation, guardianship?
Do you have anxieties about the future and your responsibilities to your brother or sister?
How has your sibling with a disability influenced your plans for the future, such as your choice of career and so on?
How do you explain your brother or sister to others?
Can you talk to friends and family about your brother or sister?
Do you know other siblings?
What are your feelings about having your own family?

inability to express any negativity as a child. Over time she came to realise that you can indeed love someone *and* be angry with them at the same time. Others have discovered that they allow a partner to 'walk all over them' or feel that they don't deserve to be cared for and cherished.

In my own relationships, I gradually came to understand the difficulty associated with expressing negative feelings, the need to be perfect and my fear of displeasing others.

Another step toward understanding for me involved recognising feelings of grief. During a period of therapy, I wrote a letter to my sister. As I sat at the computer, having written a half page, the tears started to flow. I thought they would never stop and that they would engulf me. I cried for her, for me, for my parents. And yet, in some ways, I still hadn't identified the feeling as grief. It took me even longer to see that much of what I had bottled up inside was indeed grief. It had been such a disenfranchised grief; a grief that no one ever mentioned. Through reading and talking with others, I was finally able to understand.

Many people have difficult childhoods. There are a range of reasons why children grow up with fears, uncertainties and low self-esteem. As adults, there is little point in dwelling on these and wallowing in self-pity and blame. However, there is a need to examine the difficult experiences, identify the pain, sit with it and understand it. This starts the healing process. Getting in touch with true feelings, either through reflection, reading or therapy can be very difficult and painful but, in the long term, leads to greater freedom. The pain may never go away, but it can help if you understand and recognise the feelings as they arise: the grief, anger and guilt.

For Josie, the process of reaching understanding was similar to mine.

> **If someone asked me three years ago if I had any negative feelings associated with my family and my brother, I would have been shocked. I wasn't dealing with all of these issues and feelings then. I was living my life as I thought I should, making all my decisions based on what a 'good' daughter and 'good' sister would do. But there was an unsettling feeling that I always had, as if something in my life was unfinished, untrue, fake. I was leaving things buried deep within me because, if brought up, they would cause pain, heartache, arguments, discomfort, hurt feelings – everything that I strived so hard to avoid.**
>
> **When I met my fiancé, things started to change. Much to my dismay, thoughts and feelings that I had pushed deep down inside of me were making themselves known. With a little encouragement from my fiancé, I began talking about them to him and him only. These were my terrible secrets (my guilt, my anger, my sadness, my resentments) and there was no way that I would ever tell anyone else.**
>
> **Later I had this urge to find information on sibling issues. Having contact with other siblings helped me. It was like a part of me was found. I have been trying to uncover the 'real' me, the one that has stayed buried for so long,**

scared of disappointing others, scared of hurting others. It is hard. I have cried more in the past 18 months about my brother and my family than I have in my entire life. I have been more angry with my family than I ever have before. I have been on an emotional roller-coaster, with all of these buried feelings coming out – the feelings of a three-year-old child along with the feelings of a 25-year-old adult, all mixed together and needing to be heard, acknowledged and accepted.

Despite all of the tears and emotions, the result is unbelievable. I am on my way to being the true me; I am learning how to deal with my feelings of guilt, my chronic sorrow, my feelings of missing the brother I could have had, the deep, indescribable love that I have for him.

Discover your needs

Each sibling has his own story and his own needs. The first step in your own journey is to discover what you need, both practically and emotionally. Some siblings have always felt supported emotionally and need only to find out practical details about caring for a sibling in the future. Some need to determine their own risks if they decide to have children. Others have grown up with little or no emotional support and can't even think about the practical issues. Some have distanced themselves completely from their family and their brother or sister with special needs. There may be denial and a range of repressed feelings. These siblings need to understand their own emotions and reactions, and to have some way to express those in an environment where they feel safe.

Looking at your childhood and feelings and reactions from that time doesn't mean that you need to lay blame. In fact, with more understanding it might be possible for you to forgive yourself or others in your life. Even if you feel positively about your brother or sister, lingering sadness may be hindering your own growth. You may feel protective of and inspired by a sibling, but there may still be some feelings that need exploring. Many people have good relationships with their brother or sister with special needs all through their lives. Practical problems can, however, still stir up emotions. These problems might be caregiving responsibilities, ageing parents, or a brother or sister moving into a group home. If the childhood relationship was troublesome and never dealt with, these problems can be compounded in adulthood.

For years I went to therapist after therapist, struggling each time with what I needed to do. I would be given behavioural techniques such as taking deep breaths when the panic took over, or making my 'self-talk' more positive. These approaches always left me feeling worse because I didn't seem to have it in me to change. I felt I let myself down and let the therapist down too. If I sensed any impatience or annoyance on the part of the therapist, that just added to my inability to change. I felt totally inadequate. There was never any real discussion of my family experiences.

Some siblings can benefit from cognitive-behavioural techniques, which focus on changing the way a person thinks and behaves. These approaches may have helped me too if they had been carried out in a more nurturing environment and in the context of my family background. Most therapists I saw meant well but had no understanding of sibling and family issues. Such inadequacies in therapeutic intervention cost me a huge amount of anxiety and money.

I realise now I didn't need to *do* anything specifically. What I really needed was simple guidance to help me to understand my reactions – grief, guilt and anger – and to feel accepted for who I was, and gain support from others in the same situation. Once I understood the feelings, I needed to express them. I needed to understand that by exploring these feelings I wasn't being self-indulgent or disloyal to my family.

Not everyone needs to see a therapist. There are other resources that can assist you to recognise your needs, start to address them and feel stronger in the process. See the resources section at the back of this book for some ideas.

Most siblings who do see a therapist do not require intensive therapy. What they need is support in recognising and understanding their particular situation. Ideally that comes at a young age, so that longer-term problems are less likely to arise. However, if patterns are set and more serious emotional problems occur, such as depression and anxiety, there may need to be a more intensive therapy process. Sometimes that can be exhausting and scary, but those who have gone through it can see the benefit and look forward to a more positive future.

Debra, a successful model, grew up with a brother and sister, each of whom has Fragile X Syndrome. She talks of her own growth in understanding through therapy.

> **By keeping secrets, I created a prison I had to escape from in order to reclaim my life. And by shedding light upon the mysteries that the secrets cloaked, I discovered who I am, independent of the fears and myths I had empowered.**

Debra has gone on to write *Fragile Secret*, a book about her own journey. She talks at length about her healing through the therapeutic process, both frightening and enlightening. At one point she quotes English critic Kenneth Tynan who said, 'A neurosis is a secret you don't know you are keeping.' Having kept many secrets, Debra admits to having many neuroses to work through. Like Debra, I had no idea I was keeping secrets, and only through unravelling their complexity was it possible for me to grow in understanding.

Difficulties for siblings

What follows is a brief discussion of some particular difficulties that can arise for adult siblings and some strategies to deal with them. Through reading about these experiences you might better be able to identify your own needs and seek support to deal with them.

Anger

Anger is a common emotion experienced by siblings. It's quite normal to feel anger, but developing strategies to deal with that anger will help you move forward. With the help of a therapist, Lenore discovered that she needed to understand and accept her anger in order to find healthy ways of dealing with it.

> **My parents' response to my brother's disability was to stifle my anger both by open reprimand and silent pressure. Whenever I became angry (whether it was over being interrupted at the dinner table when trying to share something of my school day because my brother couldn't stand not being the centre of attention, or his physical attacks on me), I was told 'You have no right to be angry at him because he's retarded and he can't help it.'**

> I felt my brother knew perfectly well what he was doing when he attacked me. He *could* help it; he chose not to because he learnt he could abuse me and get more undivided parental attention that way. He meant to hurt me. I often feared he meant to kill me. But I wasn't 'allowed' to be angry over it.
>
> As a result, I buried the anger under a facade and let it seethe and inform my response to life for years, until an understanding therapist finally said: 'What a horrible family situation that must have been for you. Of course you were angry. You had every right to be angry. You *have* every right to be angry.'
>
> The therapist went on to say that I didn't have the right to take the anger out on everyone around me, but needed to process it from the basis of accepting my anger as a perfectly natural and sane response to an intolerable situation, which was a very wise and true thing to say.
>
> Siblings have a right to their anger, in whatever degree they may feel it. Acknowledging my anger as sane and healthy rather than yet another instance of being a 'bad sibling' in my parents' and society's eyes was a huge step in my process of healing the wounds inflicted by my retarded brother and my family.

Guilt

Guilt is a powerful emotion that can hinder a person's growth and development. You might have difficulty allowing yourself true happiness or feel guilt about not being 'good enough'. You might have developed self-destructive or abusive ways of behaving as a result. Rachel identified her self-abusive eating problems as being related to her feeling bad about being okay. With new understanding, although the struggle and pain are still there at times, she has been able to make progress and start to feel that she is indeed entitled to some happiness without feeling guilt.

If you can identify the guilt and accept it for what it is, you might find it easier to deal with it. We need to be kind to ourselves and not put another interpretation on it, like 'I am a bad person for feeling it'. For some people, part of this process will also involve letting go of the blame they direct at themselves and others. During therapy I realised I needed to forgive the little child that was me as an eight-year-old; to understand that she did then what she was capable of understanding then, and that it wasn't surprising that she had a whole range of mixed feelings about her family experience.

Grief

I locked up the grief about my sister. Even now, when I start to think about her, I quickly change the subject of my mind's inner conversation. I identified so closely with her that I made her pain mine. I also made my parents' pain my own. It was all too much for a young child and I tried to cut off my feelings about and toward her.

Maintaining control gives us a sense of normality. Sometimes we avoid the grief but sometimes we don't recognise it. Mourning involves risk. Also, we can build up huge defensive reactions to avoid recalling losses or painful events. We have to let the emotion out, which requires letting go of control. This, however, can be difficult until you know you have enough understanding and emotional strength to keep you from falling apart. This is where seeing a therapist or talking to other siblings can often help.

Josie says:

> **Grief is an ongoing process and it is so very important that we accept our grief and acknowledge our sadness, and just be sad for a while. We deserve that, we just need to make sure that we don't let our grief take control of us and hurt us even more.**

Anxiety

The day-to-day stresses of childhood, the pressure to be perfect, guilt and other feelings can all contribute to longer-term anxiety in adulthood. Understanding and expressing the feelings can help. Other strategies that might help include relaxation training, meditation, self-help books or cognitive-behaviour therapy. The last can help you rethink your beliefs and learn to change how they influence your thoughts and behaviour. Medication might also be an option for some people, if the anxiety interferes with day-to-day life.

Tara is aware of her anxiety around performance, especially at work. As well as therapy, she has instituted some self-help strategies that seem to be effective.

> **I manage by setting time limits within which to finish something, or by collaborating on a project. Someone else's ideas can temper my perfectionism.**

Relationship difficulties

Feelings of low self-worth can be a side-effect of perfectionism. Many siblings talk of not feeling good enough. Not only does this add to anxiety but it can affect adult relationships.

Some adult siblings recognise that they have become 'people pleasers' or that they let a partner walk all over them. This can again be related to feelings of low self-worth and a sense of needing to be helpful or compliant in order to gain acceptance and love. Through understanding these feelings, some siblings are able to learn that they don't need to be a compulsive helper to have self-worth. They can learn that it is possible to express feelings openly without threatening a relationship. A relationship counsellor can help with these processes.

Depression

Denying feelings like anger, grief and guilt, and suffering from low self-esteem, can result in depression. Again, it is important to understand and accept the feelings.

Guy, whose sister has intellectual disabilities and mental illness, describes his own journey.

> **Part of my way out of the depression was to recognise and start to deal with my deep sadness and anger about the difficult things in my life. For a long time before that I tried just to look at the bright side of things, but I ignored the dark side. That is part of how I got depressed. The depression, as awful as it was, made me realise that I had big issues that I needed to pay attention to. It isn't fun dealing with those issues around loss and grief and anger but the result of going there (with the help of others) is that I am no longer depressed and have a fuller life.**

Tara also found the support of others to be crucial.

> **I am still struggling with depression. Eighteen months ago I again attempted suicide – it was a terrifying time. What helped me then and now was the support and unconditional acceptance of friends, other siblings and my therapist. They help me feel less alone and less afraid, and they give me**

> **strength to deal with my history and consider my future. That sense of not being alone is so important to me.**

Eating disorders

Several factors contribute to someone developing an eating disorder. Social pressures, images portrayed in the media and physiological issues all come into play. Siblings, however, can develop belief systems that make them more vulnerable to eating disorders. Low self-esteem, pressure to achieve, parental pressure (this might be perceived rather than real), not knowing how to deal with feelings in a constructive way, feeling out of control and putting others' needs before their own can all add to the risk.

As an adult it is important to understand the beliefs that motivated you as a child, how they influenced the way you felt about yourself, how you behaved and how they continue to influence you into adulthood. With understanding and help, it may be possible to learn other ways of meeting your needs and to develop greater self-acceptance. Carly, who talked earlier of her own eating disorder, says:

> **As a 27-year-old woman I accept that my parents did the best they could in a difficult situation. With the assistance of a psychiatrist and hospitalisation over 12 years, I am slowly moving on with my life.**

Express your feelings

A gnostic gospel says, 'If you bring forth what is within you, what you bring forth will save you. If you do not bring forth what is within you, what you do not bring forth will destroy you.'

After gaining understanding and identifying your own needs, the next important step is to develop the ability to express and explain to others the feelings that you may have bottled up for years.

In my own case I felt trepidation about explaining to close friends and extended family what I was learning about myself as a sibling. I felt guilty and disloyal about expressing the negatives and feared that people in general would think I was being self-indulgent and selfish. My first tentative announcements to close friends and associates were accompanied by extreme anguish. At times I felt a deep sense of anti-climax when my audience didn't recoil in horror and, in some cases, didn't even express much interest. The process of giving myself permission to express feelings to others extended over a considerable period and was a significant part of my own self-therapy. Over time, I continued to test the water, and eventually was able to be more open with friends, family and even work colleagues. I had no idea I would eventually tell the world.

Josie went through a similar stage-by-stage process of gaining awareness and then expressing her feelings to others.

> My advice is to talk about your feelings. Don't be afraid to let them come out. Sure, it's hard. You'll maybe feel guilty the first time you say something bad about your mum or dad or your siblings. But you are allowed to feel that way. All people, all siblings sometimes have negative thoughts and feelings about their families – not one family is perfect – so don't be afraid to say things about your own family. Tell people who you can trust, who will listen and try to understand as best they can, but also acknowledge that they cannot understand fully if they are not a sibling. My fiancé listened. He did not judge, he encouraged me to get angry, to cry, to share all of my feelings. Regular discussions with other siblings did the same. Suddenly I was feeling validated on a daily basis.
>
> So, my means of 'dealing with it' has been to tell my story to those who would listen and not judge, sharing my feelings, and not being afraid to cry, be mad, be sad. It took me 25 years to get to the point where the 'real me' is beginning to emerge and I am not as scared about what my mum and dad will think. It's still hard, but it's worth it. I still worry about other people's opinions too much. I try to please everyone all of the time. I'm terrible at making decisions. I am a worrier. But, now that I've talked about it, I'm learning where these feelings come from and, best of all, I'm learning how to cope with them and work on them.

Steps towards self-expression

This list represents the stages I went through in my own capacity to acknowledge and share feelings. It started with some self-analysis, then formal psychotherapy (both individually and in a group) and gradually extended through research and writing. In order to begin your own journey of discovery you need to explore and reflect on your experiences, by yourself. You might not need to go any further than that, but if you do, this list might help. I have outlined the various stages in my own process, but your own order of approach might be different.

Talk to yourself by writing it down

As a start, you could write about your experiences and your reactions to them – and no one else needs to share your words. Journal writing can be extremely therapeutic. It provides a private, safe avenue to express, sort through and make sense of your feelings. You could use the issues listed in the box earlier in this chapter to help you get started. I combined the writing with counselling, but you might find writing for yourself is enough to help you identify your needs and deal with your feelings. There are other possibilities too. Music, art, sculpture or dance also allow for this type of expression and can be equally therapeutic.

Talk with a therapist

If you are worried or confused by your feelings it can be helpful to see a counsellor or therapist. This doesn't mean there is anything 'wrong' with you. It just means that as a child you may have had some difficulties to cope with that would be helpful to explore.

Some siblings feel guilty about seeking therapy but try to allow yourself to ask for help. Look for a therapist who is familiar with sibling issues. That may be difficult, but disability organisations or your general practitioner may be able to help you find a suitable person. Reading this book may have helped you to explore some of your feelings and you could share them with the therapist. Not only will this be helpful to you but also to other siblings who seek help from the same therapist.

Often siblings don't need fancy therapeutic techniques; it is more a case of being listened to and validated in a nurturing environment. But it is important to recognise when a particular brand of therapy is not suited to your needs. It is easy to blame yourself for therapy not working but it may be that the therapist is not able to provide what you need.

Therapy can be painful and positive outcomes are hard won. You may have all sorts of barriers to overcome. Just because it is difficult does not mean it should not happen. It is not only the therapy but also your commitment to therapy that leads to success. Tara says:

> **The therapist who finally helped me spent more time nurturing me than engaging in miraculous techniques. Much of the first 12 months of therapy involved tears. I would arrive at an appointment full of defensiveness and bravado, he would speak and I would burst into tears for the rest of the session. He would call me between sessions and I would cry. I would think about the sessions and I would cry. Such grief, anguish and pain. If nothing else, therapy has been such a release of emotion and experience for me. I understand that these emotions were not expressed for almost 30 years of my life.**

Sometimes it is helpful to understand why we developed certain patterns of behaviour as children. The behaviours might seem dysfunctional now but at one time they helped us through difficult times.

A therapist can help you modify the belief system through which you view the world. For example, you may have subordinated your needs by not expressing anger toward your brother or sister. You may have done this because you did not want to risk the security of your relationship with your parents. A therapist can help you understand and express the anger in ways that are not threatening to you or others.

One young sibling had extensive therapy during her teen years that helped enormously. She talks of a childhood where she regularly acted up to gain attention, felt considerable rejection from her father in particular and experienced many of the feelings common to siblings. The therapy helped her to incorporate the difficult aspects into her life and be able to see some positive ones. She can look back on her family situation and see that she has become stronger and more positive through her experiences. She takes nothing for granted in life, has gained empathy for others and devotes much time to helping others in the community.

Talk with other siblings

Other siblings will understand your feelings like no one else. They won't tell you that you should or shouldn't feel a certain way. Through the interaction you will be able to incorporate the more difficult parts of your experience. You can start to let go of the secrets and gain comfort from those who share the same.

Josie joined an internet-based discussion group with other siblings.

> **The understanding is hard to explain. For me it was as if I wandered around for 23 years knowing that something was off, deep inside of me. I felt I wasn't really understood or at least I didn't understand a part of me. I knew it was there, I knew that of course I had some 'issues' from having a brother with a disability, but I didn't really know how to describe them. I joined the discussion group and for the first year I was constantly e-mailing with stories of the pain, joy and guilt that I felt about my brother, my mum, my future, my life. I feel like I understand a part of myself that I hadn't really before. I also know people who understand me when I say things about my brother or my family, or my fears about the future . . . my guilt, my sadness, my happiness. People in the group know what it is like to have a sibling with a disability in a way that no one else does – not parents, not service providers, not really anyone who hasn't had a sibling with special needs.**

If your brother or sister is involved with a disability organisation, try to make contact with siblings through that. You could join a discussion group on the internet, where you can communicate by email – see the resources section at the end of this book.

As part of Siblings Australia I set up a small one-off discussion group for adult siblings. We could have continued chatting for hours. Not only did we find it empowering to share a range of experiences and feelings that others understood, we also found it useful to share some of the practical concerns we had about our brothers or sisters. We were able to share information about accommodation options, recreation and medical issues.

You could get a sibling group started if none exists in your area – use local newspapers or radio to advertise. There are no strict rules for such a group, and meetings can be as frequent or infrequent as the members choose. Some adult sibling groups in the USA have provided information and support to members for many years.

Some siblings will be nervous about going to a first meeting. You need to ensure that it provides a non-threatening environment. As a group you need to determine what the purpose of the group will be. For some groups, the focus might be purely on gaining information about practical issues and how to access relevant resources. Others might provide more emotional support. Participants need to be clear that this is not a therapy situation, but more a process of mutual support. Each group needs to set its own guidelines.

You might choose particular themes for your meetings. These might include:

- Practical issues like accommodation and recreation options.
- Legal issues, such as guardianship.
- How your brother or sister has affected your relationships with others.
- Resources in the community to support your caregiving role.

Contact Siblings Australia (listed in the resources section at the back of this book) if you would like further assistance.

Talk with your partner

A close relationship can sometimes be the catalyst for looking at sibling issues. For example, some siblings learn to recognise the problems they have with communicating their feelings. Others identify other unhealthy patterns. However, in some cases, new understanding can be very threatening to a relationship and having counselling as a couple can be helpful.

In many cases, a close relationship can give you permission to explore the issues and release some of your secrets. As Josie found, it was the ability to talk with her fiancé that enabled her to gain understanding and acceptance.

Talk with your parents

Sometimes parents find it difficult to talk with their able children about these sibling issues, especially if the family has avoided discussion over time. Opening discussion can be hard but persistence, sensitivity and patience will help. You could give your parents books that deal with sibling issues and then start conversations based on what the author has said. Talk about the support programs that exist for siblings and how people are recognising the needs of siblings.

Acknowledge how hard it must have been for your parents and emphasise you do not want to direct blame, that you are merely trying to make sense of your own feelings. Tell them you just want them to understand your experience and acknowledge that there are difficulties for you. It may take some time before they are ready to talk openly.

Writing a letter may be a good start. Emotion doesn't get in the way so much and your parents can absorb and think about what you are saying.

If applicable, remind them they have always had each other to talk to. If you are the only able child of parents who are still together, point out that although you and they have undergone a similar journey, you have been more alone along the way.

Showing my parents parts of this book was one of the hardest steps for me. I was trying to protect them and didn't want them to feel bad about anything I had written. Talking to my parents was a significant step that opened up communication and led to new understandings between us.

If your parents won't talk at all (maybe the pain is still too great or they fear emotions might be stirred up), you need to respect this and find others with whom you can talk and sort through your feelings.

Tara eventually reached a new understanding with her father.

> **The first time I raised the issue with my family was some months after my mother died. I mentioned that I had always felt inadequate compared to my brother in my mother's eyes. I was very surprised when my father acknowledged the isolation I had felt as real and said he had tried to make up for it by including me in things with him. I wish I had known he was aware earlier – we could have spoken about it and I would have felt less alone. Anyway the conversation started some real healing between us.**

Talk with your own able siblings

If you have other able siblings in your family, try to talk to them. Like no others, they have shared in your experiences. Even though you may have had very different responses to those experiences, you can be each other's best support.

Unfortunately, that doesn't always happen. Sometimes unhealthy patterns of communication are set up in childhood that lead to each sibling taking on a different role within the family. Barriers are set up that hinder communication and sharing. For example, one may be the 'good' sibling, another the 'bad' sibling. Try to understand how that happened and try to open up the communication so you can understand how these patterns developed. If you respect your differences you can be a wonderful source of support for each other.

It is impossible to change the past. Sometimes the damage done to relationships is too great to allow any closeness. However, there are times when renewed understandings can lead to attempts to break down barriers.

I hope that the understanding you may have reached through reading this book will allow you to renew connections, both with siblings and parents, rather than build more obstacles.

It is important not to blame yourself but also to get beyond blaming others and to recognise that, like you, in most cases they were doing their best in a difficult situation.

Talk with other relatives and friends

Try to talk to other people who are closely involved in your life. Aunts, uncles, other extended family or friends can support you. The more social support that is in place, the easier it is to cope with ongoing stresses.

During the initial stages of my group therapy, I talked to a cousin who had shared large parts of my childhood with me. For the first time I discussed my fears, panic attacks and therapy. As I spoke with him, I was in a knot the whole time and, for some time afterwards, felt guilty and anxious. I still felt that I shouldn't have talked with him about such things. I worried that I was betraying my parents and my sister, and feared that my cousin would think that I was just looking for attention. We talked later on the phone – he didn't sound surprised or disapproving, just interested and keen to help.

Reaching out to another person and confiding my feelings was one of the most difficult feats I have ever managed. It was also the first step in breaking down the isolation and moving towards self-acceptance.

If you are still at school, initiate discussion with teachers or a school counsellor. They may know of other siblings in your school. They may have suggestions for services that could help you find support and create networks.

Toward the future

Caring for a brother or sister

You may not have a close relationship with your brother or sister with special needs. Try not to feel guilt about that. The development of the relationship will have depended to a large extent on the special needs of your brother or sister and how your family dealt with the situation. If you were abused as a child, you have the right to walk away if that is what is necessary to protect your life or sanity. Lenore, who lived in fear of her brother for most of her childhood, says:

> **My experience, I hope, isn't common, but one of the things that can make me feel very alone is the 'Oh, of course I will care for my sibling no matter what' pressure, and the loneliness of having stepped outside the Good Sibling Caretaker category and become the Bad Sibling who says: 'No, *my* life and sanity will not be sacrificed, I have done what I could in seeing my brother placed in a good facility, but I will *not* be pressured to go further.'**

If you haven't already done so, talk to your parents about their expectations for the future. Think about the role you will play and let them know at what level you wish to be involved. Show them the sections in chapter 10 that deal with such issues as guardianship and estate planning. Encourage them to create a file with all the necessary information about your brother or sister.

You can gain practical support from a range of people, both within and outside your family. It is crucial to have support from service providers who work with your brother or sister. Ideally, these connections are made during childhood; however, if that hasn't happened, you can still try to find supportive professionals as an adult.

If your brother or sister is involved in a disability organisation or another health service, seek out people who are willing to work *with* you. As Cassie, who oversees the care of her brother, says:

> **Over many years, I have come to trust seasoned professionals with lots of hands-on experience. I interact differently from parents, who often accept supervisors who just offer them services that sound great. As someone in more of a peer relationship, I'm more hands-on too. This year I have been dealing directly with a home support supervisor for my brother. He assists my brother in his own independent living arrangement. This person is confident enough to listen to my ideas and use me as a peer – such a contrast to the agency that tried so hard to follow its own paper guidelines, and had so little common sense, and certainly no humour about its own role. They related to me as someone outside their professional system.**

Several siblings I spoke to suggested their role would be easier if they had someone to advocate for them, who could help with accessing services and resources and who could help with problems to do with accommodation and other issues. Many siblings are not involved in discussions and planning from an early age and can find it difficult when they do take over some of those responsibilities. Again, try to access help through disability organisations or through other adult siblings.

For many siblings, the responsibility for a brother or sister feels like a heavy burden. Indeed, when I allow myself to think about the future, the feelings can overwhelm me. For much of the time I tend to take a head-in-the-sand approach, knowing that I will take over the responsibility when I need to.

As I write this, one sibling I know whose father is dying is thinking about how to include her older sisters, both of whom have intellectual disabilities, in the funeral and other aspects of the grieving. Will she need to care for them to the extent that she cannot do her own grieving? She is constantly asked, 'Don't you have other siblings who can help with all this?' She doesn't, and she is realising that she is reaching another difficult stage in her life.

Starting your own family

If you have concerns about the likelihood of having a child of your own with special needs, seek out a genetic counselling service. These services are available in each state and your general practitioner can refer you.

Of course, the results are not always conclusive, and there will be a range of issues that will affect your thinking. Information, however, can help you to come to a decision. Counselling may also help you sort through your thoughts and emotions. It might also help to talk to other siblings – some who have had their own children and some who have decided not to. Ultimately, though, it will be your decision and no one can really influence you.

Helping younger siblings

It can be enormously rewarding to help facilitate or contribute to groups for young siblings. As a sibling, your unique situation and experience can be of real benefit to such a group. Explore ways you might be able to help, either through disability organisations or Siblings Australia (for contact details, see the resources section in this book). Keep in mind that each person has a different experience. You can't assume that others will have the same feelings as you, whether positive or negative.

If you have younger, able siblings, encourage them to talk to you. Be aware that their feelings may be different to yours but that you can both gain by sharing.

At the very least, try to raise awareness of the issues for siblings. As siblings, it is up to us to talk about these concerns and to advocate for more services for families and children. We are in a unique position to improve people's understanding.

Summary

As an adult sibling, you might find the following strategies helpful in your journey toward self-acceptance.

- Try to gain understanding about your reactions and feelings.
- Think about what you need in order to move to greater self-acceptance.
- Read relevant literature on sibling issues.
- Write about your feelings toward and about your sibling with special needs.

- Share your experiences and feelings with others around you, including other siblings, family and friends.
- Seek counselling if the issues seem too difficult to sort through on your own.
- Develop a network of friends, family and professionals who can help you cope with issues that arise in the future.

10

Stronger parents – stronger families

Through the stories of siblings we discover that their experiences are varied. Many factors affect their adjustment to their family situation. Significant factors include how you, as parents, cope and the messages you give your children. And that depends on your own inner resources as well as the support you are able to access.

This chapter will give you a range of ideas on how you can become stronger. Some of these focus on you as an individual; some focus on mutual support with your partner, if applicable. Stronger parents are more likely to create stronger families, ones in which all members are more able to support each other. This chapter also looks at accessing support from outside your family.

Before we look at ways to help you feel stronger, it is helpful to consider the broader effects on you and your family of having a child with special needs.

The broad picture

Having a baby can bring enormous joy. But even when a baby is healthy, the disruption to family life and the changes in roles for each family member can bring considerable stress. Many marriages go through a period of reassessment as partners change their focus. Lack of sleep and uncertainty can lead to vulnerability, even post-natal depression, in mothers. Fathers can feel neglected, unsure of their role and anxious about their increased responsibilities. Siblings can feel put out and not sure if they really want this new little being as part of their family. When a child is born with special needs the stress and intensity of these emotions is magnified.

Each family has its own way of functioning and interacting. A family can be seen as a system. Each member of the family affects each of the other members, and the family as a whole. It's like a piece of machinery that shifts and then adjusts to those various shifts. The ongoing stress of having a child with special needs can affect how well the machine operates. It isn't so easy to function with strength and optimism. The day-to-day juggling of appointments and activities with a wide range of care providers can be exhausting and puts considerable strain on family functioning. It can be difficult for family members to interact positively with others when each feels pulled in so many different directions. There might be a breakdown in communication and the ability to support each other. The whole family system can become out of synch.

If you are a sole parent you will have your own, particular set of difficulties. You may have no one with whom to share feelings and experiences. You may have less respite from the day-to-day care demands. You will have an even greater need of support from other parents, family, friends and service providers.

There are many factors that influence a family's adjustment: cultural background, financial resources, religious beliefs and social support. In addition, the temperaments of individual family members will affect how they each adjust. Some people have great inner strength; others are more vulnerable. People perceive what is happening around them in different ways.

It can be tremendously difficult to be all things to all people. Your own reactions to the disability – which might include a vast array of uncertainties, stresses and sorrows – will affect how you interact with your marriage or life partner, and also affect the relationships between you and all your children, and the relationships between the siblings themselves. Your reactions alter the connections outside the family too – with grandparents, other extended family and friends. These effects continue over a lifetime. Some people will be enriched, others will struggle, but all will be touched in some way.

The impact on parents

As a parent, your response to having a child with special needs will depend on your beliefs concerning disability, as well as factors mentioned above, such as cultural and religious beliefs.

The type and severity of the disability will also affect your reactions. Some disabilities have more stigma attached to them and some are more difficult to explain to others. Some are more socially acceptable, which makes it easier to include the child in social interactions. Some disabilities take a long time to diagnose and such delays can lead parents to question their parenting competence. Even then, the diagnosis or prognosis may be uncertain. Some disabilities require more constant care, leading to a greater disruption of routines. If you suffer sleepless nights, your coping abilities will also be affected.

When your child is diagnosed with a disability, you may lose many of the hopes and dreams you have for your child, and you face an uncertain future. You can experience a grief that is largely unrecognised in society. Most people normally experience a range of anxieties related to the meaning of life and their own mortality. When a child is born with or develops special needs, these anxieties can be intensified. Parents might feel disillusioned and vulnerable.

You may have fears for your child with a disability, fear for yourself and the other members of your family. You see your caregiving role extending indefinitely into the future – perhaps until you or your child dies. You may struggle with anger and myriad feelings. One minute you might be feeling so protective of your child you would be willing to give up your own life if it would stop his suffering. At low points you might secretly wish he was dead. You may feel overwhelmed with guilt. Your self-esteem may be shaken.

One parent may need to cease or reduce the amount of work outside the home. Along with medical costs associated with your child's special needs, this can result in a marked decrease in family income. With reduced finances it might be more difficult to afford practical support, such as respite care and help with house cleaning.

The ongoing stresses involved in day-to-day care are often emotionally and physically overwhelming. Negotiating service systems can be demoralising and exhausting.

You may feel challenged in your religious faith, and even feel powerless and out of control. Some parents struggle with feelings of failure, incompetence and worthlessness.

All of these changes can lead you to feel isolated from the outside world. You may even lose friends and other social networks because of the demands of caring for your child. Old friends may feel left out and powerless to help. It is often difficult to take part in the recreational activities open to other families. Grappling with a wheelchair, providing special meals or dealing with exceptionally difficult behaviour can be too much to handle and it may seem easier to stay home in familiar, safe surrounds.

Joy, the mother of a young daughter with multiple disabilities, including epilepsy, talks of her difficulties in actually leaving the house.

> **I got to the stage where I avoided going out with Sally because of the tantrum she would have when I tried to get her into the car. This was physically and emotionally exhausting.**

Being with others can bring additional pain, too. A mother with an only son who has multiple disabilities but who asks, 'Why can't I play football with the other boys?' avoids the sadness caused by socialising with parents whose sons can enjoy the sport. The awkwardness that so often occurs around a family with disability adds to the family members' feelings of being different. Others don't always know what to say and often say the wrong thing. It can be difficult to know how to respond.

Awkwardness leads people to distance themselves. Joy found that mothers at the mainstream kindergarten her daughter attended avoided talking to her. Many parents talk of feeling under intense scrutiny from other parents when their child 'acts up' in the supermarket or other public place. It can be even more difficult when the disability is less obvious.

Sometimes inappropriate things are said within the family. One mother of a newly diagnosed child with disabilities had to listen to her mother-in-law say, 'This has never happened before in *our* family.' These sorts of reactions add to the parents' sense of inadequacy.

Society's pressure on parents to produce a 'perfect' child who achieves effortlessly from an early age means that producing a 'less-than-perfect' child – especially a visibly disabled one – can lead to feelings of self-doubt in the parents, along with a sense of having lost stature in other parents' eyes.

Much of what we see portrayed in the media about parents coping with disability implies that they are 'true saints' or 'specially chosen', and that, while there may be sadness in having a child with a disability as part of the household, the experience is overall a wonderfully enriching one. The reality, however, is that often families are in real pain – yet find it difficult to admit that pain to outsiders because of the messages society gives. It can seem that the only permitted response to having a child with a disability is one of cheerful self-sacrifice, and that expressing pain or anger or any other negative emotion is unacceptable.

Caroline, whose young son has multiple disabilities, including heart problems, sometimes feels frustrated by the attitudes of others. She doesn't need pity or false praise. She needs others to understand and support her.

> **I don't want to be seen as a supermum. I want everyone to know how hard it is for me.**

Caroline decided she couldn't go through with another pregnancy and so she and her husband have chosen to have only one child together. Her intended family structure has been replaced with another reality. For parents who do continue to have more children, the pregnancies can be full of emotional turmoil.

Many parents feel overwhelmed in the early stages following a diagnosis of their child's disability but, in time, most are able to say they regained their sense of control and were able to move forward in positive ways. One mother, Jane, says:

> **Of course I wish my son didn't have his disabilities – it makes his life so much harder – but the journey I have shared with him has enriched my life in ways I could never have anticipated. I have become more gentle with myself and others; much less quick to judge. I really understand, in my heart, that we are all different in so many ways and not**

more or less worthwhile because of those differences; and that we all have a right to a place in the community and can make our contribution in a great variety of ways. I understand more about the importance of being embedded in an interconnected, interdependent social network – giving and taking as we are able, and as we need, at different times and in different ways – rather than trying to struggle on alone.

The impact on a marriage or long-term relationship

The response of parents will be influenced by whether they are in an ongoing relationship and how strong the relationship is.

Stress, exhaustion and conflicting emotions can put strain on even the best of relationships. If there are problems in the relationship already, a child's disability may be the straw that breaks the marriage's back. With one parent needing to spend considerable time providing care for the child with a disability, a spouse or other children can feel neglected. Whole routines change, centring on the child with special needs and, in the meantime, it is enormously difficult to nurture the relationship.

Partners may have different ideas on the best type of care for their child. They may have different ways of dealing with the mixed feelings that arise. One partner may be able to articulate feelings easily, while the other one may withdraw. As parents, you may deal with your grief differently and at different stages.

Fathers, in particular, may feel society's pressure not to show emotion. They may need more time before they are ready to discuss their reactions and feelings. If they are not as involved in the day-to-day care of the child, it may take longer for them to acknowledge or recognise the extent or implications of the disability. All of these reactions can add to the stress within the family.

On the other hand, a strong relationship can sustain both parents through the stress of diagnosis and ongoing care, providing you both with practical and emotional support. Some couples find their partnership is made stronger through the experience of parenting a child with special needs. The whole family is brought closer together and they are able to grow in a variety of ways.

The impact on siblings

A child with a disability may make considerable demands on your time and energy, but if there are other children they too will have needs to be met. You may be less available to your other children, both emotionally and in practical terms.

Siblings of the child with special needs are, like all children, yet to develop understanding and emotional maturity. It might be difficult for adults to deal with what is happening but it is probably even more so for children in the family. Your adjustment will affect how you express feelings, give information to children and answer their questions. The way in which you deal with stress and disappointment will influence how your children deal with those things. If you have difficulty coping with your child's special needs or if you develop a negative attitude to life in general, this will be conveyed to other members of the family. As a result, siblings may act up or develop other difficult behaviour that adds to the stress and reduces your ability to cope. This in turn adds to the distress in children and the family system can break down further.

You may recognise the needs of your other children but find it difficult to respond to their feelings. Sometimes, if you are struggling with your own grief and acceptance of the changed situation, it isn't easy to identify the signs of distress in your children, who may in turn hide their feelings to try to protect you. Some siblings have said they could only share feelings when they felt their parents were strong enough to cope.

Helen Featherstone, the mother of a boy with multiple disabilities, and the American author of *A Difference in the Family*, reflects on the difficulty in acknowledging the concerns of siblings.

> **Parents care deeply about the ways in which a disability has touched the lives of able-bodied sisters and brothers. As a parent myself, I know that as much as mothers and fathers wish to understand their children's viewpoint, we shrink from the less pleasant side of the truth. We want to believe that our normal children have grown wiser and more compassionate through the family's trials. If we must acknowledge that they have suffered too, we would like to believe that this suffering is not our fault.**

The responses of siblings will be influenced by the reactions of those around them, as well as by the nature and severity of the disability, age factors, and the number of children in the family. These factors are considered in more detail in chapter 11.

Identifying your needs

Caring for a child with special needs has its own particular stresses that can continue for a lifetime. In order for you to cope, all the members of your family need to work together, often with health professionals, to identify the resources within your family and the ways in which you can help each other. Try to identify what supports are needed from outside the family – both formal and informal, and practical and emotional.

Some families will have strong inner resources to draw on, while others will need more support from people outside the family. A healthy family has a balance of both. In addition, each family member will have different needs, and these will vary over time.

As parents, you need information about the disability or illness, and how best to manage not only your child with special needs but also the rest of the family and their established routines. You need to know how to access services that will support your parenting – from both within disability organisations and within the general community. Health professionals can link you to appropriate resources. Respite, transport and special allowances can all add to your family's ability to manage.

As well as knowledge about the practical details of caring for a child with special needs you need emotional support.

You need to grieve for the loss of the child you dreamed of and planned for, and then get to know the child you now have. You may feel frustration, shock and anger. Without the opportunity to talk, the feelings can be intensified. You need to learn to communicate openly with your partner about the feelings you are likely to experience. Eventually you are likely to create more positive meanings for what is happening to your family.

You might benefit from contact with other families who have had similar experiences and who can provide reassurance and hope. You also need a range of social support from extended family, friends and social groups in the community. A

Your family's needs

The following questions might help you to think about your family's needs.

Who makes up your family? What are their interests and routines?
What are their respective skills and strengths?
What do you enjoy doing together as a family?
Are you able to share feelings with each other?
Do members of the family show appreciation, caring and commitment to each other?
How do you try to solve problems?
What meaning do you put on the disability? Do you see it as a challenge, as a tragedy, as an opportunity, or as a punishment?
What types of information and services have you received about the disability?
What has been most helpful?
Who is a part of your social network?
What support do they give you?
What are your goals for your family?
What do you think your family does well?
What particular things do you need support with?

strong family usually has a wide social network. You might need help to identify and utilise these informal sources of support.

Try to think about the emotional and practical support you need. Consider where to obtain those supports – from within your family, from professionals, and from friends and extended family.

Support from within the family

In a strong family the bonds between each member are solid; there is a feeling of respect and caring for each other, and it is easy to feel supported. A strong family enjoys doing things together, works on problems together and shows commitment to each other. There are routines for daily activities and clear guidelines for how each member behaves and treats the others. This doesn't mean that everything is smooth sailing, but a strong family has faith in its ability to cope. Some of the strengths will be inherent; others will need to be developed over time by working together and with others. The following is a list of important steps you need to take in order to move forward. If you are in a committed relationship you can support each other through these steps. Once you are stronger yourselves, you can then more readily support your children.

Make time for yourself and your partner

Caring within a family comes first from parents. In order for you to develop a nurturing environment you need to care for yourself and your relationship. That can seem overwhelming but it is important to consider the following.

Make sure you have time for your own activities, rest, fun and friends. Part of looking after yourself involves setting limits. Trying to be all things to all people can put enormous strain on your well-being. If you appear to be coping well, you might be called on as a resource. This can add to your feelings of competence but be careful not to take on too much. Recognise physical exhaustion and anxiety and, if necessary, seek help. It is acceptable to acknowledge that you are not coping. Some professionals may pressure you to deal with therapies according to a timetable that is unreasonable. Don't feel you have to keep going with such a routine if the stress is too great. There may have to be some compromise. Your most important role is to be your child's parent, not a therapist.

Stephen, 33, a father to Michael, two, who has multiple disabilities, discusses the issue of time for oneself:

> **I spoke to the psychologist at the disability organisation that supports Michael. I was having a lot of trouble accepting that Michael wasn't going to be normal. They were able to assure me that the range of feelings I was experiencing was normal – that validation really helped. They were also able to point out a few constructive coping strategies and helped us avoid a few pitfalls by warning us in advance.**
>
> **One thing they stressed was the importance of looking after ourselves and that it was okay not to focus always on the child with disabilities.**

If at all possible, find help with domestic chores like house cleaning, babysitting, transport and cooking. Having a child with special needs can put considerable strain on the family budget and so it might be difficult to afford such help, but try to find low-cost cleaning or family or friends who are willing to help out from time to time. Disability organisations can let you know if there are other services you can apply for.

If you are in a relationship, make time for you and your partner. The stresses can be enormous. Ensure you have opportunities to spend time alone as a couple. A healthy relationship can be your best support. It can seem difficult to schedule time alone with each other with all the new demands being placed on you. However, it is important to try.

Putting time aside to spend with children is important too. In families where there is a child with special needs, it is easy to overlook the other children and their desire to spend time with parents. It doesn't need to be huge amounts of time but all children need the opportunity to feel special by having time alone with parents. Formal and informal respite, as well as support from family and friends, can enable you to put this time aside. This is discussed further in chapter 11.

Communicate with your partner

People in strong families are able to communicate effectively with each other. Parents in particular need to be open with each other. Sometimes it is extremely difficult to express feelings, especially painful ones, such as grief, anger, blame or guilt. Again each partner at different times may try to protect the other. But to move forward you need to share feelings, information and decision-making. The main thing is to keep talking to each other. If the feelings seem too intense, writing a letter to each other in the early stages and talking about thoughts, feelings and fears may help. Humour can sometimes help, as long as it doesn't replace the healthy expression of feelings.

On first learning of a diagnosis, parents don't just go home with all the information and adjust. It takes time to process the information. This was highlighted by the experience of a father mentioned earlier, who spent weeks staring at the evening sky before he was ready to share anything. Fathers, in particular, may need help to reach out and open up. Some of your feelings may be quite intense and you may need to choose how to share those feelings, and with whom. You may feel pressure to be strong, but it is okay for you to admit that life hurts sometimes and to share feelings.

Parents' reactions may change over time, and you may act a little like a seesaw, providing support to each other at different stages. If one parent is reacting with obvious outward emotion and the other isn't, a divide may develop between the two. Sometimes the partner who appears to be coping and 'getting on with it' can be struggling as much, or even more, than the one outwardly expressing most of the emotion. In this situation, each parent can feel unsupported at particular times, leading to pressure on the relationship. This divide can be bridged with information and time. Knowing the other person may be in pain, even if it is being expressed in a very different way, can help some people.

At different times, you may feel pressure from within your relationship to increase communication with your partner, but often the pressure will come from people outside of the relationship. While communication is important, there can be times when people have too much to deal with themselves to be able fully to absorb and understand what a partner is experiencing, or to be able to share their own thoughts. Accepting that it is reasonable not to be communicating all the time can be a great relief and takes a huge weight off people's shoulders.

One mother, looking back, had this to say:

> **I don't actually know what my husband was really thinking about at that time, because we weren't talking about it. He was thinking and I was talking and crying. And I still really couldn't honestly say what he was thinking at that time. And that's not a negative thing, and I guess I've come to accept that. I don't need to know that now.**

Parents may have difficulty in being open about their feelings in relation to their child because of guilt. It is possible, however, to express the not-so-good feelings without devaluing the child with special needs. It involves expressing the frustration in relation to the seizures, or the hospital visits, or the amount of time spent on treatments, in ways that are not directed at the child. It is helpful for siblings to see how you do that so they can emulate you. There is some more information on this in chapter 11.

It is also helpful to share information with your partner. Joy talks about the importance of including both parents in medical appointments.

> **As the primary caregiver I had chores to do with Rose – I took her to the doctor, I dealt with her seizures, and I gave her medicine. In some ways my husband was excluded. I would go to meetings with service providers and he would keep asking me questions afterwards. I sometimes felt in the middle and unsure of the answers. After a time he organised his work commitments so that he could come to some of the appointments. It was much better when he had involvement too. It helped him come to terms with what was happening.**

For some couples, counselling can help develop open communication, skills in solving problems together and ways of supporting each other. Professional counselling can also be helpful when problems and issues that were there before learning of a child's disability become more intense and problematic. This form of support can provide a link between parents and help each to understand what they need to do.

Recognise the grief

As parents, you may take time to come to terms with your new life. You need to grieve for the child and the future you thought she had, and then turn to this child and your shared future. Grieving will help you separate from the dream and gain the strength to deal with changed circumstances.

The grief experienced by parents is often difficult to acknowledge and express to each other. But when families are able to acknowledge and express the pain and loss, they are better able to support each other, gain strength and confidence, and reach a point where they appreciate and value the child with a disability.

The sorrow can return at various times. Apart from the initial diagnosis, other difficult times can include when the child fails to reach developmental milestones at the expected times; transition times between pre-school and school, and school and post-school options; and moving into supported accommodation. Even if you feel positive about yourself and your child's progress you can still experience times of sorrow. This is quite usual and, hopefully, as parents and as a family, you can support each other through these times.

One mother said that whenever she sees a family with two daughters who seem about as different in age as her two, one of whom has disabilities, she feels teary again. She feels like telling such families to cherish what they have and not take it for granted.

Find meaning

With support and time, it is possible for you to gain a more balanced perspective on your child's disability. The child becomes a part of your life instead of the whole of it. She can be seen to have added to your family in many ways. Together as parents you can start to appreciate your own and your child's achievements, and begin to restore your self-esteem. You may learn you are strong and capable and be more able to make plans for the future. You may also be more able to recognise when to seek help.

How we cope with situations can depend on the meaning we give to them. For example, some parents may perceive the child with a disability as a punishment meted out to them for their own transgressions. Others will see the child as a gift to cherish and care for. Many will be unsure of what the meaning is for them. Part of the process may be accepting that life is imperfect and that we don't have all the answers. As parents you will, over time, develop meanings that make sense to you. Some families need support from others before they can feel positive and hopeful, but support from within your own family is crucial.

Many parents say they were able to find new meaning in their lives when they eventually reached out to others and found they could help in various ways – by reassuring new parents, or becoming advocates for people with disabilities, or studying for a new career related to disability. This can take time, however, and you need to nurture and care for yourself first.

Support from outside the family

Many families need help to be able to undertake the strategies described in the previous section. If your family is able to seek help from professionals, other families in a similar situation, and friends, you will be more likely to cope.

Professionals

You need to build your own support system of professionals, including those involved in the direct care of your child and also social workers or psychologists who might support your family. Over time, it is possible to determine which providers are the most helpful. Some will improve your ability to access information. Some will be able to give emotional support. The right person or group of people can help you improve the support within your family by teaching you ways of communicating more effectively and finding time for each other. They should be able to help you feel more competent and more able to deal with the different feelings you will experience. They can help you develop more positive meanings around what is happening and put you in touch with appropriate resources and services.

Information

There are many sources of information you can access: the internet, books, other parents, disability organisations, child health organisations, hospitals. Check the list of resources at the end of this book. Knowledge about the particular special needs of your child, and what others have found helpful in supporting their child, will help everyone in your family feel more capable.

As well as information about the disability, your family also needs to know about the systems it will need to work with, the services that are available, and sources of support. You may need different services and information at different times, as your response to the disability changes. In the initial stages, when you are perhaps full of despair, you may not absorb some of the information given to you. You may need to have it given to you again at a later stage or in a different form.

It can be overwhelming at times to feel you are the source of information for the whole family. It may be helpful to ask some of the professionals working with your child to speak to other family members directly, giving them an opportunity to ask all their questions.

Some parents find it useful to collect information in a ring binder and to write down questions that they want to ask of professionals. Service providers can support you but ultimately it is you who will need to take charge. You will become very knowledgeable about your child and your input is as important as that of anyone.

Emotional support

Part of feeling supported is sensing that others understand. Families can often be intimidated by professionals and feel they are seen as just another case. You need to be able to tell your story without guilt. You need to be able to show emotion. You need to be able to talk about your fears for the future, both for your child and your family. If you are shown understanding, you are more likely to be able to identify and ask for what you need. It is a matter of developing trust.

Professionals at support organisations or hospitals should be able to help you identify and accept all your feelings, including grief. They can help you understand the nature of chronic sorrow – that it is likely to recur during different periods – and help you prepare for those times.

If you feel the professionals you come into contact with are not able to give you this support then keep trying to find people who are helpful. Try first to address this with the professional with whom you are working. You could say something like: 'I'm not sure you are hearing me.'

Feeling competent

Parents often need help to rebuild a sense of competence and confidence. In the early periods following diagnosis, it is easy to feel totally lost and out of control, especially given the many decisions that need to be made about options for the care of a child. Professionals should be able to help you gradually regain your sense of control and self-confidence.

Professionals are starting to understand that parents have unique knowledge about their child with special needs and are starting to include parents more in decision-making. If you have contact with a disability organisation or other health-care facility, ensure that they know and understand the principles behind family-centred care.

If you feel frustrated with the support you are being given by providers, go to a higher level of the organisation. Many agencies attempt to be family-centred but sometimes they don't wholly live up to their ambitions. It is up to parents to keep pushing for their needs to be met.

You can learn practical skills to improve your competence and your ability to support each other, such as stress management, communication skills, problem-solving skills, ways of dealing with the reactions of others and assertiveness skills. Some parents are able to use difficult times to learn additional coping skills. Of course, your ability to cope may go up and down at different times.

You can also learn strategies to help the development of the child with a disability. We know that developmental disabilities lead to life-long functional difficulties. Some programs or treatments claim to offer a cure. Some parents may feel guilty that their child's lack of response to these treatments results from their own lack of energetic application to the program. Try not to blame yourself for the lack of cure or progress when, in fact, it was never going to be possible (instead, it may be the program or treatment that isn't suitable).

Parents can sometimes feel that others blame them for the problems they have. Keep in mind that sometimes it is necessary for professionals to ask a lot of questions. It doesn't mean they are trying to lay blame. It is important to focus on managing the situation as it is.

As time goes on, one parent, often the father, may have a limited ability to attend doctor and therapy appointments and so may not have as many opportunities to discuss the disability and its implications with others. This can lead to a father (for instance) lacking confidence and competence in working with the child and the system, and further distance him. Some fathers have said they feel that service providers actively exclude them, preferring to talk to the mother if possible. Mothers can also sometimes exclude the father. It is up to families, and fathers in particular, to ensure their role is not diminished.

Stephen talks about his struggles with being the father of a child with disabilities.

> **Guilt is a major issue for me to deal with. I feel obligated to go to work and support the family but guilty for leaving Michael, and to a lesser extent his sib. I struggle to find the time to spend with the kids and constantly feel guilty when not with them. I'm sure it's the same problem faced by dads of 'normal' kids but more extreme because of the extra work required by Michael.**
>
> **My self-esteem also took a beating. I'm certainly not as cocky as I was. I'm also less capable in my work. It is impossible to invest so much in work. My advice is to step back and take a less stressful job if possible.**

Access to available services

Families that have adjusted well and been able to develop strength and competence have usually had access to relevant services and supports through disability or other organisations.

Years ago, children with severe disabilities were placed in institutions. Now more often children remain with their families. Appropriate services are usually available, but not always. The search for treatment and the related frustration and disappointment is a major theme for many parents. It is easy to get on a roundabout that spins you around medical, paramedical and 'alternative' programs and treatments.

There are services out there but families often don't discover them until way down the track. In the early stages a professional from a disability organisation or hospital should become a case manager for your family, collaborating with and coordinating different services. Over time, you should be able to develop the confidence to take over that role.

If you have a problem with some aspect of the services provided, you may hesitate to complain for fear it will rebound on your child and affect the care given. This, of course, should never happen, but if it does go to a higher level within the organisation. You have a right and responsibility to make a reasonable and respectful complaint. If the organisation practises family-centred care, where you are seen as valued members of the treatment team, this is less likely to be an issue.

Respite care

Families need respite to recharge their batteries from time to time. It is important for the family as a whole and each individual member, including the child with a disability, that parents have some respite. You might use the time to spend with your other children, to watch them play sport or go shopping. You might use it to spend time with your spouse. Or you might use it as time out for yourself.

It can be exhausting to negotiate the service system, and you may not always have the energy or confidence to do this on your own. Some parents feel guilt about seeking respite. Remember that people in families with able children have respite from each other and no one thinks twice about that. You are caring for a child who years ago may have been institutionalised at a huge cost to taxpayers. Instead you are providing that care and you have a right to respite. At the same time, it can be difficult finding respite care with which you feel comfortable. You deserve an opportunity to reassure yourself that the respite providers are competent and caring.

Respite is of enormous benefit to the siblings in your family. It can also enrich the life of the child with a disability by allowing her to develop some new relationships and some independence – after all, sleepovers are a normal part of a child's life.

Respite time can include weekends away for the child with special needs, a paid carer in your home for, perhaps, two hours a week, holiday programs and personal-care support. The best respite is the one that is designed to meet your family's needs. It may include paid workers, services support or extended family members. Ask other parents who are in the same situation what they have found useful.

You need to start the process of respite in a gradual way so that all members of the family can become accustomed to it. It is good to start when the child is young, initially with small amounts of respite time.

Some respite options have a long waiting list, so try to plan for the future. One mother discovered that a respite cottage used by families at her child's special school had a waiting list of two-and-a-half years. Put your name down as soon as possible.

Unfortunately, many families struggle to gain respite because of funding restrictions. It is easy for governments to find the money for more glamorous projects – supporting families in need of a break often takes a back seat. One family with whom I worked closely had become cynical and depressed after years of trying to gain some respite from their young son with autism. They wanted to spend just a little quality time with each other and their younger daughter, who was struggling emotionally. The funds weren't there, they were told. I gave the emotional support I could, but what they really needed was time alone – and that would cost money. It is easy for such families to feel that no one cares or wants to know.

Both service providers and parents need to advocate for more respite to be available, as well as other practical services like transport and equipment. As one mother said in a recent media article, when discussing the lack of respite for families:

> **Nobody sees the long-term cost of not dealing with this problem now, that there could be five people – not one – on their welfare books as a result of a family falling apart. If taxpayers only knew, I think they would be happy to deal with it here and now.**

Other parents

Parents are on their own journey, but other parents who share similar experiences can provide enormous reassurance and practical suggestions. Often they are the best source of support, especially given that the relationship between you and the other parents is based on equality and empathy. They can show you that it is possible to make it through the often overwhelming feelings to the point where you know you will make it.

Other parents can show you how you will eventually be able to see your child as part of your family, rather than the whole of it. They can share what they have found helpful, both within their own family and in dealing with the service system.

Some parents may be quite unhelpful because of their own unresolved issues of grief or anger. Some may impose their own attitudes and create more fears, so be selective and spend time with the parents you find most helpful.

Meagan, a 23-year-old sibling, says:

> **Over the last six years most of our real support – emotional support – has come from other families in the same situation and not from the professionals at support agencies. It's a**

> **shame that even though help is out there we had no idea that it existed, let alone how to obtain it.**

In the United States a widespread Parent to Parent program trains veteran parents – those who have had similar experiences but who have been able to move forward and develop strength and confidence – to make contact with parents of a newly diagnosed child with a disability. This program gives enormous support to parents at a time when they most need it. Sometimes it is an individual parent, sometimes a couple, and sometimes a whole family that makes the initial contact. Single parents can benefit from such interventions, too. Most times in the USA it has been parents who have been the main initiators of such programs. With help from professionals they have been able to use their own experience to ensure families are able to access appropriate support in the very early stages and move toward a more optimistic outlook.

Many groups exist in Australia and elsewhere where parents get together for discussion or social activities. Again, these groups can give you practical and emotional support, and reduce your sense of isolation. They will help you develop your own coping skills and a more positive view of yourself and your child with a disability. Some organisations bring together whole families to share support. Stephen says:

> **The disability organisation also runs a dads' get together occasionally. This helped because by meeting a few blokes with disabled kids I worked out that I wasn't unique.**

You need to learn ways of dealing with the reactions of others, and other parents can often help with that. It is reasonable to feel uncomfortable about the ways in which some people respond to you. They may use dismissive clichés, such as 'You were specially chosen for this' or 'God only gives what he knows you can deal with'. They may stare or make unreasonable judgements. You can learn ways of responding (or not responding in some cases) that will help you feel more confident and comfortable. You can help other people to understand in the process. Sometimes humour, if used appropriately, can help. Deborah Fullwood and Peter Cronin's book *Facing the Crowd: Managing other people's insensitivities to your disabled child* gives a range of ideas on how you can deal with others' reactions.

This is a valuable book, not only for parents themselves but also for parents to share with their children. In addition to helping you understand your own reactions and those of others around you, the authors suggest a range of strategies. One chapter deals specifically with managing clichés.

If you choose to respond, the book suggests it can help to ask yourself a series of questions. Examples include: 'Will I see this person again?' 'Will I hear this again from someone else?' The answers might help you decide on your response. It might be different for a person you like and see often than for a stranger. I particularly like one response suggested for the cliché above about being chosen by God: 'God has chosen *me*? I wish He had asked me first.'

Friends and extended family

Seek out friends and family members who can support you and who make you feel good. In some cases it will take time and may not be easy but, if you can find people who will give support, you will feel much stronger. The support networks you need often change over time in response to your changing needs, your family requirements and your child's development.

Parents may need help to discuss the grief with others, especially their children. Parents often feel the need to put on a brave face in an effort to protect their children from the pain. Some do the same with grandparents and close friends, but extended-family members and friends need permission to grieve too. Caroline talks of the mutual support she shares with her best friend.

> **My closest girlfriend cried, and continues to cry, with me. We have been friends since kindergarten and always dreamt our children would be friends too. We mourn the fact that my child will never play as we had planned with her children.**

Another mother knows that the first day of a new school term is always difficult for her – her son is unable to attend the local primary school with all the other neighbourhood children. On each occasion she meets a special friend for lunch to help her get through the day and her renewed sorrow.

Some family members may find it more difficult to accept what is happening because they are not dealing with the issues daily. Grandparents often come from a generation where disability was viewed very differently. They may feel grief on two levels – both for you and your child, and for themselves – and they may have difficulty in giving you full support in the early stages. If they are included in discussions and encouraged to be open, they are more likely to be able to be there for you. It might help to have a trusted service provider talk to extended family as the need arises.

Without social support, families can become increasingly isolated and find it difficult to cope. Support from friends and the extended family acts as a buffer and helps all members of a family cope and feel stronger and more valued. This kind of informal support can increase your confidence and make it easier for you to access more formal types of support through professionals.

Stephen, a father, mentions the benefits of being able to accept help.

> **Another thing that freed up a lot of time is that my dad does a lot of simple house repairs and gardening for us these days. My mum does similar things to make my wife's life easier. We've both gradually learnt to accept a bit more of the help that's offered. If we didn't have the help then a lot of things just wouldn't get done. Believe it or not, one day my wife asked my dad to fix a busted light I hadn't gotten around to replacing – he replaced that globe and another 12 blown globes around the place!**

You may find you become isolated from friends and family and you may need help to recover and develop these relationships. Service providers can help you gain skills to do this. You need to learn ways of communicating with friends and family about the disability and ways to ask for help.

Other informal support

Other groups within the community, such as church, Scouts, Guides and sporting clubs can all contribute. It can help a family to belong to a group in which all members of the family are included and valued. List the groups you belong to now and try to investigate other options as well.

When families are supported in appropriate ways, often they are able to gain control, develop strength and a sense of competence and security. The rewards can be many and such families are able to see, looking back, how their lives have been enriched. As one mother says:

> **Siblings' and parents' lives are changed forever, but those changes, although unwelcome at times, can be avenues for growth. Many families become involved in community groups, provide support, education and inspiration. When the dust has settled, shock resolved, routine of life established, joy can be found in unlikely places.**

Early in this chapter one mother, Jane, reflected on what she had gained from having a child with special needs. She goes on to say how support from her family and community has enriched her life and helped her cope.

> **The early years after the diagnosis were very tough, and I needed professionals to help me understand the difficulties my child had so I could understand the difficulties he faced and better appreciate his abilities.**
>
> **I found the support from other parents of children with disabilities invaluable in the early years. That was where I felt most accepted and where I learnt not to judge.**
>
> **My family of origin has been vital for my well-being over the years, offering both emotional support and much-needed practical help. For years I found it hard to trust anyone other than close family to care for Nick and give me a much-needed break.**
>
> **As Nick has grown up, I have felt the importance of taking our place in our local community. Of learning about the ways members of our family can contribute, and helping others to see the value of allowing us to do so.**
>
> **As time goes on I know how essential it is to focus on ways of caring for myself and for important relationships in my life. I used to concentrate so much on the details of what my son required each day that I had no time or emotional energy left for anything or anybody else. Now I have a much better balance. Nick's needs are important, of course, but so are my daughter's, my partner's and my own. Other members of my family and friends also have needs that take priority at times and I am no longer racked by guilt when I don't get around to things I 'should' do for Nick. I do the best I can**

> **and feel confident and secure that that is sufficient and that there are many other people who make other enriching contributions to his life that complement mine.**

Planning for the future

Discussion within the family about future plans for the care of the person with special needs is crucial in the development of a stronger family. It can be extremely difficult for parents to consider the future when they may be trying to deal with each day at a time. It is important, though, to consider what will happen when you, as parents, are no longer able to care for your child with a disability. Not all siblings will want to be involved in those discussions, but many will.

Planning needs to occur well before the death of a parent, as it can be particularly difficult for siblings to find out all they need to know about a brother's or sister's care, when they are also coping with the sadness and stress of losing a parent.

Many siblings have said that they wished their parents had written everything down for them – health information related to the disability, contact details for doctors and dentists, and financial information. Parents often don't want to burden their other children but it is helpful for siblings to understand expectations and have some knowledge of what will be needed. It can be frustrating for siblings who understand and accept their responsibilities if parents fail to acknowledge the siblings' roles.

Consult widely, particularly with a lawyer and/or the disability organisations that support you and your family, as well as trusted friends, in order to work out the best plan for your family. There are various resources available, including the internet. The following are some issues to consider.

Accommodation

Finding suitable supported accommodation for a person with a disability can be a worrying and difficult process. If suitable accommodation can be found, however, the benefits will be enormous for all concerned. Adjustment is certainly easier when the person can have regular contact with parents – on weekends or for holidays. Such arrangements allow the person to start to develop some independence and to form other relationships. Parents and other family members gain respite, which allows them to contribute more positively. And perhaps most importantly of all, the person with a disability is doing what other people do – she is leaving home.

The person with a disability may still be living at home when a parent dies, and subsequently have to move. In some cases, these families have had no contact with a disability organisation that could support them. It can be an extremely stressful transition for the person to have to move and at the same time adjust to the loss of a parent or parents. Equally, it can be difficult for siblings to deal with all the necessary arrangements during their time of grief.

My parents wisely followed advice to place my sister in a group home when she was in her thirties. Although they experienced much grief and guilt about carrying through the decision, the outcomes have certainly been positive all round. For a long time my sister protested whenever it was time to return to the group home after a weekend visit, but gradually she has adjusted and now returns quite happily. My parents still worry about my sister, but the level of support they receive from the disability organisation is very reassuring. It certainly allows me to feel more secure in my future role knowing that she is settled and cared for.

Guardianship

Some people, because of reduced mental capacity, are incapable of making their own decisions. There are legal processes in place to protect people in this situation.

Each state will have something equivalent to a Guardianship Board that can make various orders depending on the needs of the person with the disability. The two main types of orders are Guardianship Orders and Administrative Orders. The Guardianship Order gives a person ('the guardian') the right to make health and lifestyle decisions on behalf of a person with a disability. An Administrative Order gives a person or a trustee company ('the administrator') the right to make legal and financial decisions on behalf of a person with a disability. In both instances there would need to be evidence that the person with the disability is having some sort of difficulty managing their own affairs.

Siblings may have responsibility for a brother or sister with a disability and it is best if they understand their various legal rights and responsibilities. Again, consult with a lawyer, disability organisation or the relevant state authority.

Estate planning

Planning for the distribution of assets upon their death can be a difficult process for parents. This may be more complicated when a child with a disability is part of the equation. Planning and decision-making, however, can have a huge bearing on the quality of life of all your children.

The nature and severity of the disability will affect how the future is planned. Particular consideration will need to be given to the way in which a child's disability may affect their ability to manage their own affairs. Many physical disabilities and health impairments will not preclude a person managing their own financial affairs. If employment opportunities are restricted or there is a chance of deteriorating health for one particular child, this may be taken into account when deciding how to divide an estate.

One important consideration is whether the person with a disability would lose government benefits should they be left a substantial amount of money directly.

Many parents set up a trust fund that can be managed by an appointed executor. Sometimes there might be two executors, such as a lawyer and a family member, who manage the trust together. In some cases, a trust fund is set up before the death of parents; it is then simple to transfer the management to other parties.

For peace of mind, it can be helpful if families consult a lawyer who has had experience in estate planning, particularly where one of the beneficiaries is a person with a disability.

Journal of life

It can be helpful for siblings and others who are interested in the care of the person with a disability if parents keep a journal of the life of the child concerned. The journal could document a range of historical information about the child and give some thoughts, ideas, plans and suggestions for the future. The journal could, for example, have sections covering the past/present/future in the following areas:

- Accommodation and living arrangements
- Education and employment

- Health care/medical
- Social/recreation
- Particular likes and dislikes eg food, recreation etc
- Added expenses associated with the child's disability
- Behaviour management techniques that work best
- Useful services and resources available in the community which could include particular organisations and individuals (such as 'Aunt Maud, and Mr Bennett, at x address are great supports . . .')

Conclusion

The support that you are able to access outside your family will certainly influence how each family member will cope. In the end, however, it is crucial that you are able to learn to provide that support to each other.

Debra Lobato, in *Brothers, Sisters, and Special Needs*, concludes that it is the characteristics of the family itself – the way people feel about one another, talk to each other and cope with stress – that play a major role in sibling adjustment.

> **Siblings do best psychologically when their parents communicate their expectations and feelings openly, talk about the illness or disability honestly, do not overburden them with childcare and household responsibility, and manage to maintain pleasant and supportive marital relationships. While these family styles of coping do not make the sadness of a child's illness or disability disappear, they do seem to enable brothers and sisters to develop some of life's most admirable personal qualities.**

Summary

Much has been written in recent years about strengthening families – 'empowering' them. In a strong family the members are able to seek help from one another, from professionals and from family and friends. You will be more able to adjust positively if you are able to:

- Identify the needs of *all* members of the family.
- Access information about the disability and the system you will be dealing with.

- Be involved in decision-making concerning your child with special needs.
- Learn to communicate and share feelings with members of your family.
- Gain emotional support so that you are able to understand your feelings, feel more competent and develop more positive meanings for the situation.
- Access practical supports and resources through professionals, other families and your social network.
- Make plans for the future care of your child with special needs through discussions with professionals and your whole family.

11

Stronger children

We have read about the experiences of adult siblings and gained insight into the impact that growing up with a disabled brother or sister can have on a child.

These stories teach us the importance of providing support to siblings as early as possible, and continuing that support throughout their childhood. Some siblings seek counselling in later years to help make sense of their confusion. Their experiences and feelings as children are explored, and through a process of validation these siblings may become more self-accepting and appreciate whatever positive effects they have experienced. If this process can begin at a much younger age, the future for the sibling and the family is likely to be far more positive.

We need to help siblings, as children, to recognise and acknowledge their role in their family and their own needs. You will read in this chapter a range of ideas on how you, as parents, can support them. Many of the approaches can be used to improve communication and sharing of feelings within your family, and to ensure children grow up feeling competent, cared for and important.

The adjustment of siblings is governed largely by the way parents handle the situation. Whether a child grows up with security or anxiety depends on whether they have someone who listens to and validates them. Loving and caring sometimes are not enough. Once parents understand the needs of siblings, it can be relatively simple to provide support to able children. There may be other adults in a child's life – aunts, uncles, grandparents, friends – who can give that support too.

Whatever the situation, if children feel safe, supported and valued, are able to share information and feelings, and feel they can solve problems, make choices and have some control over their lives, they will develop greater self-esteem, strength and resilience. Sometimes a sibling of a child with special needs will find these attributes difficult to develop. With the right type of support from an early age, however, their chances of adjusting positively are greatly enhanced.

When Emma, an 11-year-old with a 15-year-old brother who has cerebral palsy, was asked what were the good and bad things about having a brother with disabilities, she wrote:

> **I guess a good thing about having a sibling with a disability is that you develop more of an understanding about things than a person who has not got a sibling with a disability.**
>
> **Another good thing is that my brother looks up to me because I know a lot of stuff he doesn't.**
>
> **There are many bad things, too, such as my brother will sometimes attack me because he simply can't get his message across to me, so I feel hatred towards him. Sometimes I feel jealous of him because my parents make a lot of fuss over things he does and not as much fuss over things I do.**
>
> **But, hey, if you think about it, these feelings are just the same as a child would have if their sibling didn't have a disability, so it isn't that much different after all. I would say the good feelings are love and friendship and the bad feelings are jealousy, hatred and frustration.**

Emma is able to be philosophical about her role as a sibling. She has been given permission in her family to express the not-so-good feelings and, in so doing, is able to recognise the positive side of the relationship with her brother. She also has significant social support, which not only provides validation for her as a person, but also reinforces the idea that her brother is valued and cared for.

No doubt Emma will face challenges in the years ahead but she feels secure and supported and has developed a strength that will help her meet those challenges.

Identifying needs

Each child will react differently to a brother or sister with a disability, and so particular needs will be different. Each family situation is complex and the needs of children must be explored in that context. Children's needs change according to their stage of development. They will also go through different phases. Even the most caring of siblings may go through a period of intense embarrassment and want to distance him- or herself for a while, especially when friends are visiting the family home.

It is important that siblings gain support from an early stage, rather than waiting until problems arise. If behaviour signifies a problem, it is important to look at what the behaviour means and assess what the child needs. It is also important to understand that a quiet, so-called 'easy' child is just as much at risk of distress as a child who exhibits difficult behaviour. Parents and teachers often overlook these children because they don't disrupt daily activities.

If there are only two children in the family, a sibling may find it difficult to learn basic social skills. In some cases, during the early years, siblings may think the behaviour of a brother or sister with a disability is the norm. Younger siblings use an older brother or sister as a model of behaviour. When the other child has disabilities that affect his or her behaviour, the younger child may be confused. Increasing siblings' access to extended family and friends and participation in a variety of social activities will help them develop necessary skills.

Some siblings, especially where the special needs of their brother or sister are very demanding, will lack attention from parents, and families will need to work out ways of trying to correct the balance. Other siblings might need to learn ways of interacting more positively with a brother or sister with special needs. Some will need more information; others will need to be relieved of some of the responsibility they have been given.

Sole parents may feel particularly worried about the support they can give their children. However, you can feel reassured. Much has been written to suggest that children are more likely to develop resilience and self-esteem if they have a close, enduring relationship with one significant adult. And there may be other adults in their life, beside the parent, who can provide such a relationship.

When exploring the needs of siblings it is useful to focus on the areas where they need the most support. Parents and service providers can then work together to provide that support. Other people with whom the family comes in contact, such as therapists, teachers, adult friends and family members, may also be enlisted to help.

Strategies to support siblings involve helping siblings to feel strong – that they are competent and valued, and know that they are not alone. They need to be able to balance thinking of their own needs and the needs of others. Most adult siblings tell us that as children they needed to be included in discussions about their brother or sister with special needs. They needed to be able to express all their feelings, and to feel loved and important within the family.

Consider what resources are available within your family to nurture and support your child. Then check the supports and resources available outside your family, both informal and professional.

Supporting your children

Let's look at specific ways in which you can support your children who are siblings of a child with special needs.

Encourage open communication

Without open communication within a family, everyone gets bound up in a cycle of protecting each other from real feelings. This only adds to the intensity of those feelings. It is difficult enough putting on a mask for the outside world without feeling it necessary to do so inside the family as well.

Most times, children can cope with stressful situations if they feel listened to and understood. You might want to arrange a regular family meeting that gives all family members the opportunity to share feelings, questions and information in a supportive environment. If you feel you need help with this, a social worker could get you started. These meetings can also help a family to discuss expectations and plans for the future. On the other hand, some children respond more when given regular time to talk with an individual parent.

If there are two or more able siblings in your family, help them understand they can support each other with their own particular concerns.

In the next few pages I describe some ways to help your children communicate more openly.

Share information

Clear information, at their level of understanding, helps siblings to feel more secure. You may try to protect your children from sadness or fear, giving the message to a sibling that he is too young to understand or that she 'doesn't need to worry about that'. But children *do* worry. They create their own interpretation of the feelings they sense around them. Children are influenced by both the spoken and the unspoken feelings of parents. Accurate information can prevent children making false assumptions and developing irrational fears and worries.

Ensure that siblings know they cannot 'catch' the disability and tell them whenever the opportunity arises that they are *not* the cause of the disability or illness. These reassurances are vitally important in building a sibling's confidence in interacting with both the child with special needs and peer groups.

Siblings need to know where the child is when they are in hospital and who is looking after them. It can help if they are actively involved at certain times in the care of the child with the illness and if they can be reassured about their own role in the family.

The information you give children needs to be tailored to their age. Young children don't need to be overloaded with information – simple explanations are best. If you are unsure of the facts yourself, this needs to be communicated to children, and information then sought from a range of sources. Books about disability that can be read together with children are especially useful. Doctors or other professionals can also be asked to help explain the situation to siblings, provided they give an explanation at the child's level of understanding.

Joy found one strategy useful for opening up communication, not only within the family, but also in other settings. She and Rose put together a book about Sally's life.

> **When Sally started kindergarten, Rose and I put together a book called *Sally's Story*. We got a sketchbook and wrote about Sally. We included what she enjoys doing and described her wobbly walking and delayed speech, her epilepsy and what children could do if she had a seizure. We wrote the book**

Identifying a sibling's need for support

To identify the needs of siblings and plan their support, it can be useful to consider the following questions. Does the sibling:

Understand his brother's or sister's special needs?
Choose to spend time with her brother/sister?
Want to include his brother/sister in family activities?
Teach her brother/sister new things?
Experience feelings such as sadness, anger, embarrassment?
At times resent the time parents spend with the child with special needs?
Seem withdrawn?
Show signs of trying to be the 'good' boy or girl?
Show signs of being an overzealous helper?
Seem to act up a lot, with difficult behaviours?
Have sleeping problems or physical symptoms like stomach-aches?
Seem happy at school?
Seem able to answer questions from others about his brother or sister?
Have a range of social contacts with friends and extended family?
Take part in recreational activities outside the family?

using simple language and lots of photos of Sally doing things like other children her age. Not only did this book help us to talk about things together, it also helped in a number of other ways.

1. **It explains Sally's problems to the children at her kindergarten.**
2. **It includes Rose in a project to understand Sally's problems.**
3. **It gives Rose the words she needs to explain to her friends about Sally.**
4. **It explains/reinforces to Rose's friends that they cannot 'catch' epilepsy.**

Using labels

Some parents try to protect the child with a disability from the diagnosis by not using the name of the disability. Some parents don't feel comfortable using a label. If siblings pick up your discomfort, they might be confused by the mixed messages. Using a label can be helpful to able siblings and the child with special needs in the following ways:

- Your children will eventually hear the diagnostic label from someone else and you will have to deal with their reactions then.
- When we don't use diagnostic labels it makes it seem as though they are so horrible that we can't even speak about the disability. Sometimes what we don't say conveys more of a message than what we do say.
- By providing a diagnosis, the problem is somewhat depersonalised in a good way. Particular features or behaviours are no longer specific to the individual. It makes him part of a group of people who have similar behaviour and problems, but he and his siblings will not feel as though these problems are his alone. This can help the adjustment of all children in the family.

Answering questions

Siblings need to know that it is acceptable to ask any question that troubles them. Some siblings have said they could only ask questions when they knew their parents were strong enough. Children often need permission to ask questions, particularly about issues they see upsetting their parents. If you are struggling with your own emotions, other family members or professionals may be able to help explain the situation to a child. It is helpful if you or other designated adults (professionals the family comes in contact with, extended family, teachers) can try to provide regular opportunities for questions.

As children grow older they may ask difficult questions such as 'Why did this happen?' and responses will need to be meaningful. Each family will have its own ways of answering such questions, depending on its religious faith or view of the world.

During their teens, siblings may become concerned about having their own family. One 14-year-old girl whose younger sister has Down Syndrome was worried by pronouncements made at school about the genetic issues involved in this syndrome. They contradicted her own understanding, but she didn't feel confident about questioning the teacher. Also, she had started thinking about her own risks of having a child with a disability. A visit to a genetic counsellor (a genetic service is available in each state – you need a doctor's referral) enabled her to feel reassured not only about the broader genetic information but also her own risks.

Involve siblings in decision-making

It is important that *all* family members are included in discussions about the diagnosis and what the disability means for the child and the whole family. When decisions must be made where the needs of a disabled child take precedence over his siblings, try to discuss this beforehand.

A sibling's responsibility for her brother or sister with disabilities can last a lifetime. As siblings become older they need to be involved in discussions and decision-making at each step. If this starts at an early age it is easier to continue the process. Parents may try to protect children from responsibility but most adult siblings say they wish their parents included them more in discussions.

Young adults need to know what is expected of them, and many will want to take a more active role in decisions made about their brother or sister. Even if their brother or sister is in a residential facility, siblings can take them to doctors, dentists or other appointments, and be involved in other aspects of their care. They may end up having responsibility for coordinating services for their brother or sister. Some may care directly for a brother or sister in their own home.

Siblings need to know what their responsibilities will be in respect of financial, medical and legal issues. Some families have found it helpful to record for future carers all the details about the person with a disability. (See *Planning for the future* in chapter 10.)

Acknowledge siblings' feelings

Siblings need help in identifying and expressing the different feelings that arise. They need to learn that it is normal to have a range of feelings, including love, embarrassment and anger, toward a child with special needs. Let your child know that you understand his anger, disappointment or embarrassment. That can be difficult if you are grappling with mixed emotions yourself.

If a child with special needs hurts a sibling, it can be helpful to say something like: 'Your brother isn't able to help himself but I am sorry he did that to you and it is okay that you are angry.' Some siblings describe their frustration at being regularly dismissed by a parent with the words 'he can't help it'. You can acknowledge the sibling's feelings while still promoting understanding and compassion for the child with special needs.

Occasionally parents won't tolerate any expressions of negativity at all toward the child with special needs, even to the point where a sibling is not allowed to defend herself against aggressive behaviour.

Try to avoid telling a child how she or he *should* feel. It can be tempting to say to a young child, 'You should feel lucky you don't have your sister's problems,' but in reality we can't expect that of a young child.

If your child expresses guilt, don't try to reassure him too quickly or dismiss her feelings. Show her you understand and then talk together about what might help.

Marie, whose sister has developmental disabilities, gives us an invaluable message when she says:

> **I do think the best thing we can do for our young ones is to empower and teach them to be able to *be with* the feelings, such as guilt, that they will feel in their lives. Most seem to feel guilt. What if children were to learn to recognise the guilt, not make up other ideas of what it means (like 'I'm bad', 'I don't deserve', 'why me?'), and be able just to understand and accept it and themselves? Wouldn't that be fabulous?**
>
> **If a child is feeling angry or guilty or whatever, don't deny it. See it. Be with it, describe it, turn it over and upside down; help the child learn to accept that part of himself or herself without recrimination.**

Children need to share their feelings about anxious times. I wrote earlier about the anxiety Renee felt each time her brother was admitted to hospital. She sat and waited not knowing if he would die. Everyone else was so worried there were no opportunities for her to talk about her own fear.

Label the feelings

Try to help your children label their feelings. You might say, 'You seem sad – perhaps it is because Susie can't play with you?' or 'You seem angry today, perhaps you feel fed up because I missed your basketball game again.' Take the risk of guessing; if you make your guess tentative, children won't mind if you get it wrong and may even correct you and, in the process, talk about their feelings.

Also, siblings might not know how to express feelings such as 'it isn't fair' or 'what about me?' One mother says that sometimes her young son will come up to her and say, 'I want to sit on your lap now.' The child himself is recognising his need for some extra attention. Not all children are able to express their needs so easily and parents need to help them.

Boys can have particular difficulty with expressing sadness. We give them the message they shouldn't cry but we don't give them alternatives. Often the sadness will be acted out in aggression. Labelling the feelings can help children learn to identify the feelings that come up. They also need to learn appropriate ways of dealing with the feelings. (See pages 160–162.)

Truly listen to what siblings say

Sometimes the feelings of a sibling are not obvious. Truly listen to what children say and put yourself in their shoes for a while. The little girl who told her mother 'I wish I was deaf' didn't really mean she wanted to be deaf. She merely needed her mother to understand that she wished she could have the gifts and attention her sister received. She felt left out, but then she felt worse about herself because her mother gave her the message that she should not speak in such a way.

When you truly listen it is easier to acknowledge the feelings behind what siblings say. If your child says, 'All you ever care about is Jimmy,' say something like 'Yes it must feel that way to you. It's not how it is but I can see you might feel that way.' It is easy to quickly respond with: 'No, I don't.' But that belittles your child's feelings. It is much more constructive to acknowledge the feelings and then move on to how you can help her have a more balanced view.

Parents can usually find other adults to talk to – a spouse, other family or friends – but siblings may feel they have no one. If you are busy or preoccupied, it can be easy to feel annoyed and dismiss your child's comments. If this is the case, try to put time aside later in the day to come back to discussing what a child has said.

Watch your child's behaviour

As well as listening to what your sibling children say, be mindful of their behaviour. Children in general often develop difficult behaviour in response to experiencing difficult feelings. It is important not to assume that their most apparent feeling is the only one they are experiencing. For example, an apparently angry child might be sad or frightened. If you can see behind the anger, this might lead to unusual closeness and understanding. The earlier discussion on labelling feelings can be helpful here.

Watch for behaviour that may indicate stress. A child may become clingy or whiney or revert to baby-like behaviour. There may be changes in sleeping or eating patterns, social withdrawal, headaches or stomach-aches.

Some children might adopt disruptive or aggressive behaviours in an effort to cope with their feelings. Boys, in particular, who get the message they should be strong and not cry, learn to act out their feelings in an aggressive way. For some boys there is reduced opportunity to participate in sports, thus limiting their outlets for anger and other difficult feelings.

Sometimes 'acting up' behaviour can indicate a desire for attention. Find out if such behaviour is happening at school. Siblings may not behave in these disruptive ways at home for fear of upsetting parents, but may still try to get the attention elsewhere.

Watch for a child who regularly withdraws to cope with the stress he or she feels. A child who withdraws, has low self-esteem, or feels sad or helpless is more likely to have problems with school and friendships. Such children are at risk of developing depression. An unhappy child need not become a depressed child but watch for signs of increasing withdrawal. If you are worried, seek help from a child counsellor.

Even if a sibling seems well-adjusted and happy, he or she may still have some confusing, worrying feelings which, if left unexpressed, can lead to problems.

Be watchful for the 'good' child, the child who always seems to want to please and make things right. If a sibling keeps being praised for being 'my little helper' or for 'coping so well', it can become even more difficult for the child to disclose that in fact he or she is not doing so well.

As siblings move into teen years they might show other signs of distress, such as losing confidence or developing eating disorders.

Keep talking to your children. Most problems arise through not talking. It might be difficult and painful to address feelings such as anger, guilt or sadness, but in the long run everyone in the family will be stronger and healthier.

Parents as models

Parents need to try to be role models for their children. If parents are open and honest about their feelings, children will be encouraged to be the same. This doesn't mean 'letting it all out' all of the time. There need to be some boundaries and parents have the right to some privacy with their feelings. If siblings feel loved, however, they can cope with seeing a parent's emotion. It is possible for parents to express feelings of frustration in a way that doesn't devalue the child with a disability. For example, you might say to a sibling: 'I am so fed up with these hospital visits. I'm sure Jamie is too. How about you?' Knowing that her own parents are sometimes sick and tired of the situation helps a child to feel less alone in her own exasperation. It gives her permission to express her own feelings.

Josie says:

> **My mother was never afraid to talk to me about what a troublemaker my brother was being. She was never afraid to cry in front of me. Actually it was a blessing when my mother cried in front of me. It helped me remember that she was not made of steel, she also hurt and needed me as much as I needed her. It felt good to know that my mum did not expect me to always like him – he was, after all, my brother. You aren't supposed to always like your siblings – 'normal' or not!**

Parents and siblings can support each other if given the opportunity. Joy tells this story:

> **When Sally had a seizure at the shopping centre, Rose and I were faced with a difficult situation in front of a lot of people. When we were driving home, I said to her, 'Gee I find that sort of situation difficult at times. How did you find it?' We ended up debriefing each other.**

Such mutual support can be very healthy. This mother is sufficiently aware of sibling issues to know how to support her child. She may not get it right all the time, and at times she finds her young daughter's openness upsetting, but she is acutely aware of the need for Rose to discuss her concerns. She is able to support her young child and, although there are ongoing concerns and difficulties, Rose is growing up in a situation where she can feel good about herself and her family.

In addition, Rose has had individual counselling with a psychologist, has attended sibling groups and has a strong social support network. So she is gaining support from within and outside the family – both informal and professional. Not all children have such sturdy support.

Sometimes the roles of supporting each other can become unbalanced and a parent may need to restore roles that are more appropriate. Joy had concerns when it seemed that Rose was taking on too much of a nurturing role.

> **When Sally had her long seizures early on in her epilepsy, I would sit there in tears, treating her seizure. Rose was only about four and she would run and get the tissue box. Not for Sally, but for me! Then she would 'throw my tears away', like I used to for her. One day when this happened I suddenly looked at her and thought, 'My God, this is around the wrong way.' I didn't cry any more and gave Rose more support.**

Mothers of sons, in particular, need to be mindful not to use those sons as emotional partners, especially when a father is absent. Sometimes young boys can carry a large emotional burden in this situation.

Another important lesson children can learn from parents is that it is a sign of strength, not weakness, to ask for help.

Using language

The words you use will influence children as to whether or not they develop optimism. If you say, 'This is hopeless, we will never get anywhere,' or 'Everything is ruined,' they learn to use similar language. If you say, 'This is very difficult for us, but we will help each other, and I feel sure we can make things better,' children learn to think in a more positive way. Try to use words like 'maybe' and 'sometimes' rather than 'always', 'never' or 'can't'. Read books to young children that convey the idea of thinking positively. Try to convey hopefulness rather than hopelessness.

Creating more positive meanings

The children in your family will develop their own meaning for the situation, based on the messages they get from you and others around them. Think about the way you respond to situations; the messages you give to yourself and others. Children absorb such messages.

A child who believes that people who stare are making negative judgements may feel differently from a child whose parents introduce the idea that people who stare might be curious, compassionate or, in some cases, ignorant. A child who gains adequate attention in other ways from parents, who is able to share her thoughts and feelings, and who feels special and valued is less likely to think, 'All they care about is my sister.' She may still feel resentful from time to time about the attention a child with special needs receives but is less likely to experience constant negative feelings.

People from their social networks and support groups can also help your children develop more positive meanings, but your influence is very important.

Dealing with feelings

Once children know it is legitimate to experience a range of feelings, they also need to learn that feelings such as anger need to be expressed in a safe way. For example, it is not acceptable to hurt someone. Try to give a child alternative ways of expressing her anger, such as writing about it, talking with someone, going for a walk. Having said that, it can be helpful to allow siblings, including the child with special needs, to interact roughly. Josie talked earlier about how her parents allowed her to hit her brother if he hit her. That doesn't mean really hurtful hitting, of course, but *all* siblings play roughly at times and that can be quite healthy for everyone. (Some disabilities, though, make a child extremely vulnerable and clear guidelines then need to be set.)

A sibling may try to imitate the child with a disability, or pick up worrying ways of communicating. This may be because the sibling is identifying closely with his brother or sister, and is trying to understand his brother or sister's experience – what it feels like to live with a disability. Joy describes a particularly frightening incident.

> When Rose was four and Sally two, the girls were in the lounge together. Sally came running out to get us and pulled us into the lounge. She still could not talk very much and I knew something was wrong for her to call us in. When I walked in, there was Rose having what looked like a generalised seizure. All I could think was, 'Oh no, they've both got epilepsy.' I stayed calm and said, 'Rose, are you okay?' just in case she was play-acting. She immediately stopped 'fitting' and stood up with a small smile on her face. We didn't make a fuss in spite of wanting to shake her and tell her how much she had terrified Mummy. Instead, I left it until the next day and asked her if she had made out to have a seizure. She said yes. I asked why and she said she wanted to know how it felt for Sally. We then suggested that if she wanted to do that again, she could, but she just had to tell Mummy and Daddy before she did. Interestingly, she never did it again. We also arranged for her to talk to a friend who has epilepsy about what a seizure feels like and that seems to have fixed her curiosity.

Siblings might want to try out a wheelchair or put on splints to see what they feel like. Also, a sibling may feel she will get more attention if she acts in similar ways to her brother or sister. Try to show understanding and tolerance. The behaviour is unlikely to continue, but if it does, it may be necessary to consult with a therapist. Information and open discussion can help to resolve behaviour like this quite quickly.

It may be useful to have siblings write down feelings or to draw pictures about them. Notice when a child spontaneously writes or draws something in relation to their family. Let the sibling know you are interested and that it is acceptable for him to do this. Even if he doesn't wish to discuss it, the drawing itself may serve a useful purpose for the child. You might want to work on a story with your child or encourage him or her to keep a journal. Parents and adult siblings can also benefit from writing about feelings – that is how this book started. Other strategies include reading storybooks about disability, talking with older siblings and creating a 'story of me' book or creating a book about the child with special needs.

Attending activities just for siblings, such as groups or camps, can also be an effective way of providing a safe and supportive outlet for emotions such as anger and grief.

Help all children feel special and valued

It is easy for a sibling to feel that the child with the disability is more important. They become aware of the child with a disability gaining more attention, or getting away with difficult behaviour.

Give them time

Siblings will usually understand the extra attention the child with a disability needs if they know that they too will have some special time with you. Make sure you spend regular one-on-one time with your able child – talking, playing a game, reading together, going out for a milkshake. Marking this time on a calendar reassures the child that time together is important for you as well.

Use non-verbal strategies as well, by being there for them or letting them know in different ways that they are acknowledged. Find opportunities to watch their various activities, like playing sport, even if that means getting a sitter for the child with a disability. As one mother said:

> **Sometimes it is difficult to do this because you feel exhausted and mentally zapped from the intrusiveness of the disability, but you have to make yourself.**

In one family a sibling had developed a range of difficult behaviours. Though the mother found it extremely difficult, she bravely recognised that she felt a greater bond with the child with special needs. Gradually, and showing much inner strength, she was able to shift more of her attention to the sibling and recognise the needs of that child. Combined with individual sibling counselling, the situation improved significantly. Not only did the mother feel more connected with her able child, but his behaviour became much more manageable.

You might want to ask a member of your extended family or a close friend to take a special interest in your able child, much like a godparent would. This person can then spend time with the sibling, take him on outings and show an interest in school, friends and other activities. This can help a sibling feel valued and loved.

Attention was less of an issue for Julie, partly because she had brothers, but also because she was given the message that she was an important member of the family.

> **I don't remember feeling that attention was an issue, maybe because I had brothers. Also, my parents must have done a great job in spreading it around, even though the changes in our life were enormous. I do remember crying to my mother that I missed my sister being able to play. I received a big cuddle and I think I may have cried a bit more than I needed to, in order to get some extra attention. I remember too, that when I was about 15 and going through an unhappy time with teenage blues, my father came into my room and said, 'Just remember that there is something very special about *you*.'**

This father was able to show his daughter she was loved just for being her. A sibling, especially in a two-child family, will live with the pressures of feeling that in many ways he is the only one who can fulfil his parents' dreams. Try not to add to those pressures by placing heightened expectations on him. Let him know that it is not his responsibility to make things right or better for everyone, that he doesn't have to be perfect and that you love him just the way he is.

Siblings can feel especially isolated when they are separated from parents who have to spend lengthy periods in hospital with the child with special needs. Siblings need to maintain contact with you on a regular basis. Perhaps family or friends could help with visiting so you can go home to spend time with your other children.

Acknowledge the achievements of all children

Try to acknowledge the achievements of *all* your children, according to their individual interests and strengths. It is easy for parents, other family members and friends to make a huge fuss of the achievements of a child with special needs and overlook those of a typical child. Some siblings describe how their parents have shied away from congratulating them in front of the disabled child so as not to upset him or her. Try to keep a balance in recognising what all your children are achieving.

Try not to compare or create competition between siblings. Talk about how each individual has strengths and weaknesses and identify these for each family member, including parents. As Jane said:

> **After discussing my daughter's asthma with her she said, 'Mum, Nick has cerebral palsy, I have asthma . . . What have you got?' I felt a bit left out.**

Be fair

You may need to think about your parenting style. Should it be the same for all your children? For example, some children with autism need a strict, structured routine to follow. That would not be appropriate for other children in the family.

Don't keep blaming the sibling for disputes or excusing the behaviour of her brother or sister. Allowances may have to be made for a child with a disability and most children will accept this if it is discussed openly and expectations are clear. Include all children in family tasks. A child with a disability is often able to do simple chores and will benefit from this participation. Older siblings regularly say parents overprotect their brother or sister. This affects that child's ability to develop to his or her full potential and move to some level of independence. It is very easy for parents, especially the main caregiver, to become overly involved with the child with special needs, but this can be unhealthy for everyone in the family.

Try not to give more gifts or goodies to the child with a disability than to his siblings. Discourage other family members from doing this, too.

Acknowledge and value the care given by a sibling

If a sibling contributes but is not overburdened he has much to gain from helping out. Most importantly, when a sibling helps with caregiving she needs to feel the contribution is valued.

Ask agencies to help siblings learn ways of interacting positively with their brother or sister through teaching skills or playing games. When siblings take on a teaching role, rather than merely caregiving, they feel pride in their contribution. Some of the books listed in my further reading guide can help you teach siblings how to play and communicate with the child with a disability.

For example, Sandra L. Harris, in *Siblings of Children with Autism: A guide for families* gives a range of ideas for encouraging play between a sibling and a child with autism. Parents talk of the benefits to the whole family as the sibling finds pleasure and satisfaction in the interaction. Harris concludes:

> **Playing together is one of the important exercises that brothers and sisters share. It is part of building the sibling bond. When one sibling has autism that play is often disrupted by the difficult-to-manage behaviour and lack of apparent response by the child with autism. Research suggests that siblings can learn how to help their brother or sister become a playmate. A sibling who can master the basics of giving effective commands, providing generous rewards for correct responses, and offering necessary physical or verbal guidance may find that these skills change difficult interactions into pleasurable ones. A parent who is skilful in the basics of behavioural teaching can help a sibling master these skills. However, it is very important that the sibling be motivated to learn the skills and that the playtime not become a burden for her.**

Try to allow the sibling herself to decide on the level of responsibility she takes on. There needs to be a balance. Too much responsibility may lead to resentment and also hinder a sibling's move to independence. As a sibling grows older, he may be capable of taking on more responsibility but, instead, might choose to spend time with peers. Later he may decide to accept more responsibility. Never assume a sibling will care for a brother or sister with a disability – always ask. It is also important to make expectations clear. For example, is the sibling responsible or not for disciplining the child with disabilities?

Make sure your sibling child knows that he or she is just that: a child and a sibling, not another parent. Allow all your children the opportunity to *just be* children, to explore and play together. Emphasise what they have in common. Playgroups for children with disabilities and siblings can help a sibling learn ways to play and have fun with their brother or sister.

Encourage independence in a sibling

In earlier chapters I discussed the huge responsibility siblings can feel toward a brother or sister with special needs. They may need your help to realise it is important for them to develop their own goals and to move toward an independent life.

Having some space

Don't force a child with a disability into every aspect of a sibling's life. Don't expect a sibling to include her brother or sister in games with his friends all the time. It can be painful to watch your child with special needs excluded from a group, but all children experience this at times. It is important, when possible, to explain to the child with the disability that everyone needs private time, both alone and with friends. If you feel the exclusion of the child is a significant problem, then talking about it openly with siblings may help. You could negotiate guidelines for when a child with a disability is included and when not. When a sibling has a friend over you might spend time with the child with a disability to enable the sibling some space.

Ensure siblings have some privacy at home. In some cases, that might include providing a separate room with a lock, or a cupboard with a lock where they can keep possessions safe. Not only does this give siblings personal space, it also gives them the knowledge that their needs are important too. As Josie says:

> **My parents made sure I felt free to express my anger, annoyance and frustration. When it became a daily occurrence that my brother messed up my room my parents put a lock on the outside of my bedroom door so that I could lock it when I wasn't there. It was a simple hook lock but my brother did not have the reasoning skills to unlatch it. I could leave my room and not worry about what would happen. It was so thoughtful and showed such respect for me. Because of their attitude I did not grow up with any resentment towards my brother.**

Outside activities and interests

Many families become very close through dealing with the challenges of a disability in the family. This can be positive but sometimes it can be difficult for children to separate in a healthy way from their family. Let siblings know it is acceptable to be independent and encourage them to develop their own interests outside the family. Social support, especially from peers, is crucial to developing their own identity and feeling good about themselves.

The logistics of taking a sibling to outside activities such as sport practice and music lessons can be difficult. Siblings can be forced to miss some of these activities because parents are too busy caring for their child with special needs. This reduces both their social contact and their feelings of independence.

One way in which a child develops self-esteem is through experiencing a sense of mastery in what he or she does. Certainly many siblings do have the chance to develop a feeling of competence, not only through contributing to the family routine and care of a child with special needs, but also through the pursuit of various achievements. Activities such as dance, music or sport can all add to a child's self-esteem. Even if children are struggling in one area of life, such as schoolwork, these other activities can restore their faith in their own abilities and their own worth.

Try to enlist the help of other parents who might be able to share driving. In Melbourne, one organisation, Carenet (see the resources section), works with families where there is a child with chronic illness. Through a large group of volunteers, it enables siblings to develop a close relationship with an adult. This often includes attendance at activities that would otherwise be impossible.

Teen issues

During the teen years, a period of heightened self-consciousness, siblings may want to move away from the family somewhat and not be seen with their brother or sister. They will be starting to separate their own needs from those of the rest of the family, but creating their own identity can be a cause of inner conflict for them. It can be a time of increased responsibility in relation to their brother or sister, but this needs to be balanced with their own independence and identity development. Again, they need to know it is fine to become more independent and that developing friendships and connections away from home is important for them.

Adult issues

As siblings become adults, they often worry who will care for their brother or sister when their parents are no longer able. They may have concerns about leaving home or moving to another city. Families need to discuss such issues openly. Parents shouldn't expect siblings to give up their own lives, although many siblings will want to be involved at some level and will make life decisions with this in mind.

Prepare siblings for the reactions of others

Unfortunately people do stare and tease; they do so out of fear, ignorance, compassion or just plain curiosity. Children need to learn ways of dealing with the reactions of others.

Information

During a discussion group one parent commented, 'Oh, my son doesn't think his brother is disabled.' It can be tempting for parents to leave such perceptions as they are. Eventually, however, siblings will need to be able to answer questions people ask about their brother or sister, and know how to react when others stare or tease. Knowledge and understanding enable children to respond to others' ignorance more easily. They don't necessarily need to use medical terms but they need to feel comfortable with the words they use. A young child will find a simple explanation like 'his brain doesn't work properly' or 'his muscles don't work properly' sufficient to explain a sibling's unusual behaviour. As siblings get older they will need more sophisticated words. Of course, in the early stages, parents themselves sometimes lack a full diagnosis from the medical profession. It is still best to be honest and convey what *is* known.

Watch your behaviour

Your child will learn most about how to respond to others by watching your responses. Joy talked earlier about her daughter's seizure at a shopping centre. At the time she realised how much influence she had over her other daughter's reactions.

> **I had to explain to a number of people what was going on. While I was paying for the food, Rose had to sit with Sally, who was lying on a chair. When people asked if everything was okay, she responded in the same way I had.**

Susan, whose older sister has Down Syndrome, talks about her own reactions and how they changed over time, largely due to her parents' actions.

> **My sister embarrassed me. She would go up to people and hug them and I would get all flustered. I always felt I was different. I loved her dearly but was still embarrassed and felt I was being judged by others. When she and I were in our teens our family went overseas. My parents didn't let her disability interfere with what we did. Everywhere we went people**

responded to her. I became more relaxed after that, I wasn't so self-conscious. I realised that people treat her depending on how we treat her. I think it depends so much on the family and how they deal with it.

If the family seems to be comfortable and accepting, others may learn to react to a child's disability in similar ways. One family that includes a child with autism has developed an innovative way of handling stares and curious looks. They hand out cards that detail the behaviours of someone with autism and strategies for dealing with these. This simple act sometimes opens up communication and can lead to improved understanding. Instead of shrinking away and hiding, this family is reaching out, educating and enlightening others. In the process, it is reducing its own isolation. Be mindful, though, that if you do this as a 'mission' rather than in an easy, relaxed way, the effect may be to turn people away. Also, you might not always feel like talking to others about your child's disability. It is okay to say, 'I don't feel like talking about it now.'

Children can learn skills to deal with others' reactions. Parents and children can work together on responses. By pretending to be in difficult situations the child can practise various strategies. For example, as a parent, you could play the role of someone staring. Allow the sibling to try different responses and discuss the likely outcomes for each response. Earlier I mentioned the book *Facing the Crowd*, which gives a range of strategies to use when dealing with others' reactions. Once you find some that work, you can help your children to use similar strategies. Again, role-playing different scenarios can help.

Dealing with teasing

Teasing can be particularly worrisome for siblings. Again it can help to role-play situations, so children can rehearse how to respond. They might choose to ignore the taunts, or say something like, 'My brother has a disability and can't play football but he really likes computer games.' Apparently comedian Bill Cosby recommends repeating the question 'So?' in response to any teasing. A typical interaction might be: 'Your brother's a retard.' 'So?' Yeah, well he can't do anything!' 'So?' It is easy to see that the teasing is unlikely to lead anywhere or be repeated. The teaser will not gain much satisfaction from such an exchange.

The American website 'Teasetips' (see resources) has a range of other ideas and links to other sites on teasing. For example, children suggest the following: Simply ask the person (calmly and without emotion) to repeat what was said, like, 'I'm not sure I heard you correctly. Would you mind repeating what you just said?' Usually the teaser doesn't know what to do after such a comment and will either apologise or tell you to 'skip it'. If the remark is repeated, though, don't say one single word. Instead, make it a habit to always leave an insult with the person who made it. Another idea on the Teasetips website is to write down all the upsetting comments children make and with the help of others come up with some answers to use in the future.

A child's way of thinking about things will determine to a large extent how he or she reacts to teasing. Sibling groups enable children to act out scenarios, discuss strategies together and, in the process, start to change the way they think. For example, if in response to the teasing a sibling assumes, 'They reckon I'm weird,' he will feel uncomfortable and inadequate. If instead the child is able to think, 'Well, those guys tease other kids too. They're pretty mean to others too. It's not just me,' then he will be more resilient to any taunts. Talking about such issues with other siblings of their own age will help siblings feel stronger when others tease.

At times a sibling will join in the teasing directed at his brother or sister. Most of the time the sibling will feel protective, but occasionally the divided loyalty may be too much to handle. Let your child know that you understand that he loves his brother or sister but at times finds it difficult to stand up for him or her, especially when among friends. All siblings tease one another, particularly under peer pressure; it is normal behaviour. It might help if you talk about ways the child *can* stick up for her brother or sister but still feel a part of her peer group. Again, sibling groups can help children to feel stronger in doing this. Also, if a child feels comfortable, a teacher could have a discussion in the classroom on disability issues and teasing. A parent might want to be involved as well.

Acknowledge and discuss the losses for siblings

Josie says:

I wish my parents would acknowledge how sad it is for me to

> **watch my friends who have 'normal' sibs and acknowledge that I too feel sad when my brother turns five, 13, 21 etc. I feel sad he can't have a 'normal' relationship with my friends. I feel sad he can't tease me and wrestle with me, that we can't plot trouble and lie to our parents for each other and protect each other and even hate each other sometimes.**

Many adult siblings express similar sentiments. They recognise their parents' pain but feel that their own sense of loss is rarely acknowledged. Earlier in this book one mother talked of the sadness her daughter felt when her younger sister went to a special school rather than her own 'normal' school. This mother learnt to acknowledge her daughter's sadness. She encouraged her to visit the special school and gain an understanding of why it was needed. Some children will need help to understand their feelings of sadness. As a parent, you can do this by talking about and labelling your own feelings.

Some parents feel defensive when siblings talk about the negative aspects of having a brother or sister with special needs. Perhaps it adds to the parents' sense of guilt over not being able to provide a 'normal' life, or compounds their feelings of failure. Siblings will go through difficult times and no one can do the grieving for them. The role of parents, however, is to understand and provide support.

Support from outside the family

Professional help

Check the resource list at the end of this book to find where you can get specific help to support siblings. Sometimes, just talking to a service provider who is aware of sibling issues will be enough for you to gain confidence in your ability to support your children. If you see a social worker or other support people with your child with special needs, they might be willing to see the other children as well. In some cases, it is better for siblings to see someone who is less involved with the child with special needs.

Other professionals who can play a role include physiotherapists, speech pathologists, psychologists, doctors, nurses, teachers and general practitioners. Just having someone who takes an interest in them, and wants to know how they are coping, is helpful to siblings. Service providers can all help a sibling deal with feelings and reactions and put them in touch with other opportunities for support. Intervention, such as counselling, might be helpful, even if a child is not exhibiting specific signs of having difficulties. It is best if problems can be prevented.

Claire, a parent, says:

> **Parents are adults and have access to lots of information and support, although they may not recognise it as such. When a parent takes the child with special needs to the doctor, they often get support from staff, even if it is just, 'How can we help you today?' or 'I know this is hard for you etc.' Typical sibs don't have that type of support. They often get harrassed at school and by friends who don't know how to respond. I get frustrated with parents who say that their kids are okay and don't need additional support.**

Some children may develop particularly worrying behaviour, such as withdrawal, aggression, difficulty with socialising and trouble sleeping. These might all be signs that the child is struggling to cope. It can be difficult for a parent to acknowledge that a sibling is having problems and that a child may need more specialised therapy. Look for a child counsellor (psychologist, psychiatrist, social worker) with experience in working with families that include a member with a disability.

External help such as this is useful because siblings can express a variety of feelings in a safe, non-judgemental environment without fear of hurting others involved. They can also learn ways to deal with problems and start to think about their own goals. Often the relationship with the child with special needs will also improve.

Family counselling may enhance the relationship between siblings, particularly with older children and where significant problems and issues exist.

Some siblings seek therapy in later years to try to make sense of their confusing reactions. Some are able to reach a point of self-acceptance and appreciation of the positives. If this process can start at a much younger age, everyone in the family will benefit.

Sibling programs

Sibling groups

Many adult siblings wish they could have connected with other siblings as they were growing up. They would have learnt that they were not alone in their struggles.

Children may be able to get together with other siblings through disability organisations or through other families you know. Give children the opportunities to meet and then let them develop their own friendships within the group.

Innovative group programs for siblings have been developed in Australia and overseas. Some children benefit from both individual counselling and participation in a group.

Benefits of sibling groups

As well as providing information, sibling groups give children an opportunity to share feelings and experiences in a fun environment. They can start to feel more 'normal' and often start to feel more positive about their brother or sister. Such groups allow siblings to be honest about difficulties, without the fear of being judged badly. Siblings who have participated in such groups talk glowingly about the benefits.

Group sessions include activities, information and discussions about ways of coping with the day-to-day challenges experienced by siblings. Some siblings feel that they have little control over what happens. Many are at risk of developing a general feeling of hopelessness. By hearing how other siblings might deal with difficult situations, they can feel stronger and more powerful; they start to see that they can learn the skills to cope with problems. Strategies used by other siblings are likely to be more readily accepted than those given by people who haven't had personal experience of the issues. While these groups are not therapy as such, they can be quite therapeutic.

After being a part of sibling groups, children commonly express a strong desire to meet again. They make comments like, 'At least I have somewhere I can talk about things now.'

Jim, a social worker with an Adelaide organisation that supports people with intellectual disabilities, has run many groups for young siblings. He feels strongly that these groups give valued support to siblings.

> **The middle primary school years and adolescence are two stages in human development which see the influence and approval of peers being very significant in our psycho-social development. Information given to us by peers at these times in our growing up have a huge impact on our 'okay-ness'.**

> **Skilled and experienced group workers recognise that the *group* is the agent of change. Acceptance, empathy and clear information gained from peers in a group process are likely to have a larger and more lasting impact on group members than information and validation provided by group leaders or other adults.**

Some parents worry that by attending sibling groups a child might pick up negative feelings that weren't there before. Some are afraid the child might come home and say things that are distressing for the child with a disability. Other parents see the group as an opportunity to enhance openness in their children and communication between parents and children. They see it as support for them as parents too. Although it can be difficult for parents to fit meetings into a busy schedule, the long-term benefits can be wide ranging.

Feedback from parents after their children participate in such groups is usually extremely positive. Some note that siblings engage more with their disabled brother or sister. Others have said that while their children have gone to the group feeling negative, they have come away confident that they have some influence and can make choices. One mother noticed that being part of a group helped her daughter to open up and talk about her experiences and feelings. The sibling was also more able to discuss the disability with friends.

One mother had been particularly concerned because her eight-year-old daughter had been exhibiting signs of anxiety and nervous behaviour. After attending a group, the child seemed more settled and able to cope. About nine months later the child was filling in a magazine survey on the theme of friends. One of the questions asked her to identify her best friends. She responded with the name of her special best friend and then listed 'the sibling group'. The effect was greater than her mother had realised. For this child, like many, the group provided an opportunity to feel a real allegiance with others and to lessen her isolation. The mother noted that her daughter was now articulating her feelings about her brother much more readily, saying, 'It is really sad that he can't play with me.' The daughter talked about how, in some ways, she felt like an only child because she had no one to play with – but unlike an only child much of the attention was given to her brother. Being able to express such thoughts shows a healthy development in this child.

In addition, the mother told a story of how each day her son with special needs was dropped off by his school bus to the local primary school after-school care. His sister, who also went to the after-school care, always welcomed the arrival of her brother. The worker involved noted that this was quite unusual. Most of the other siblings were nowhere to be seen, pretending there was no relationship between themselves and their brothers or sisters with special needs. Again, the mother felt the sibling group had influenced her daughter's behaviour in this positive way.

Sibling groups do sometimes stir up emotions that can spill into the family home, but most times the discussion that follows is positive. Sometimes parents have difficulty coping with a child who begins to express his feelings more openly. One mother said that her child had begun to express anger after attending a group. The mother had regularly given this child the message that she shouldn't complain, that she should feel lucky because she did not have the difficulties her brother with disabilities had. No doubt the group convinced this child that it was okay to feel negative feelings as well as positive ones, so for a while she had 'let loose'. Things settled down and the mother acknowledged the child was interacting in a more positive way with her brother.

Setting up sibling groups

We all need to lobby for agencies to provide sibling services. Agencies can be given help with this through Siblings Australia based in Adelaide (for contact details see the resources list at the back of this book). The project is developing a manual for facilitators of sibling groups that outlines everything you need to know to establish a group. It gives ideas for activities, ranging from a one-day workshop to an eight-sessions group program. Also there is a list of sibling services around Australia on the Siblings website.

As a parent, you might want to set up a group yourself. Sometimes family camps are held and sibling programs can be incorporated into them. Parents in this situation avoid being in the same small group as their child when serious discussion activities are taking place. This allows the child to speak more freely. During this time the parent can be working with another small group or preparing for snack time in another area. If you don't have group skills or experience working with children you could ask a relevant practitioner to co-lead with you.

Parents have been a driving force behind many of the groups in the United States.

Carol tells her story like this:

> I am a parent of three lovely daughters, the youngest of whom was born with spina bifida. When our youngest daughter was born, my first question was, 'Will she live?' and my next was 'What will life be like for her two older sisters?' (then aged two and five). Being in the field of human development and early childhood, I knew that all of us needed support. You can't do it alone, and asking for help is a sign of strength, not weakness. Most supports were for mothers then, a few forming for dads, but not much for sibs. I had training in the Sibshop model developed by Don Meyer in the United States [see resources] and started up a group in our home town. It was wonderful, even with my involvement. When we broke up into discussion groups, I would encourage my girls to be in a different one from me. They didn't always choose that, but it was their choice. Now our youngest is 13, and the older two girls facilitate groups themselves. We also give presentations on sibs at various conferences. It has been a wonderful support to acknowledge, with our girls, the good and not-so-good parts of being a sib.

Claire also started a sibling group.

> As a parent I want to do everything in my power to give all my children a happy 'normal' childhood. The fact that I have four kids and two of them have significant needs does not mean that I want that any less. I would like my kids to grow up in a home that doesn't have all the chaos that ours does, but they can't. I feel guilty about it but I can't change it. The trick is to acknowledge that it is beyond our control, acknowledge that the 'typical' sibs also have special needs and try to look for the positives in the situation.
>
> My eldest daughter is sandwiched between an older brother with mental illness and a younger brother with developmental disabilities and emotional disturbance, and both boys have significant behavioural issues. I started a

> **sibling program for her, to provide her with a support system with peers. Is she okay now with her sibs? No, but at least she is sensitive to the needs of others, she reflects honestly on her feelings, sets limits and acknowledges that it's okay not to be okay about her brothers all the time. She often speaks to groups about sibling issues, helps out with the sibling group for younger kids (where her younger sister loves to go), and, yes, she does love her brothers. Peer support for sibs is beneficial not only for the sibling but for the whole family.**

Sibling programs with a different focus to groups have also been developed. Carenet for example, in Victoria, provides individualised attention for siblings of children with serious illnesses. Its frontline is the Co-Pilot's Program, where a carefully screened and trained volunteer is assigned to a specific child. Co-Pilots are so named because their role is to accompany the child on their journey, and seize any opportunity to encourage and build up the child's self-esteem. Richard Paterson, the founder of Carenet, says:

> **Being in their formative years, these children's experiences have a profound impact on how their personalities develop. Clearly, an ill child's requirements are disproportionately high. Most of the family's resources are focused on the ill child. The well siblings (due to their stage of emotional development) tend to perceive this as the ill child being of greater value. Other feelings often evolve, such as resentment, low self-esteem and guilt. Such feelings during childhood tend to have a detrimental influence on future mental health.**
>
> **One young man, in particular, comes to mind. His brother died of leukeamia when he was a child. This young man has a serious drug problem. He acknowledges he turned to drugs as one way of dealing with the pain.**

School

School is a major part of life for all children and can provide a further avenue for social support of siblings, both formal and informal.

Talk to your child's teacher about the stresses in your family. (Chapter 12 talks about how teachers can support siblings.)

Ask the principal if there are other siblings in your child's year level. If so, suggest that two or three could be placed in the same class. If appropriate, and if you feel comfortable, you could try to make contact with these families, where there is a child with special needs.

Suggest a disability awareness session be held in the classroom. You could ask for help from a disability organisation, but most schools should be able to provide assistance. If your child is comfortable, she could contribute to the session by talking about her brother or sister. Joy discussed earlier the sharing of *Sally's Story* in Rose's classroom.

Jane talks of her daughter's sharing at kindergarten.

> **My four-year-old daughter proudly took her brother's wheelchair to kindergarten for Show and Tell. It gave her kudos and prestige, and demystified the wheelchair. All the kids wanted to go in it.**

As children grow older, this type of sharing may not be so easily achieved, but starting such activities at an early age increases the chance of siblings feeling positive in the long-term.

Schools can also run more formal sibling groups. The value of a local group is the ease in developing networks. The initial contact may be through a formal group, but it can continue in a more informal way (see further discussion in chapter 12).

Siblings at the same school

In recent years there has been a general move to 'mainstream' children with disabilities into normal schools. This means that siblings, both able and with disabilities, often attend the same school. This can have a range of benefits but parents and school personnel need to recognise that siblings in this situation may need extra support.

Parents and school staff need to encourage siblings to discover their independence, to build personal peer networks and to achieve at school in their own right. They need to be discouraged from playing primary caregiver roles at school (remember, siblings are kids too). Earlier in the book, Susan expressed her relief when her sister moved to a special school.

Some siblings might feel that their popularity is diminished because of what they perceive as their difference from their peers. But having a brother or sister with special needs at the same school can also be very positive for siblings. It shows them that children are children first, and their brother's or sister's acceptance and inclusion in the local school reinforces that. Jane says:

> **For our family it has been wonderful having both children at the same school. My daughter's friends see her brother as an included, valued and familiar member of their school community. She doesn't have to explain his differences. It reinforces the belief that all children, whatever their abilities, belong in families, in communities and in schools.**

Informal social support

Some siblings might be in nurturing, caring families, but find that they do not have much opportunity for informal social interaction, especially with peers. Because of a child's disability, it may be difficult for his or her family to interact with other families.

In single-sibling families different problems occur. One young girl who has an older brother with autism has underdeveloped social skills. She has loving, caring parents but, without the chance to learn social skills from an able sibling, still struggles with friendships with children of her own age. Her parents are mindful of this and ensure she participates in a range of outside activities, such as drama and tennis.

It can be useful for siblings to identify their own informal support network, which might embrace parents, grandparents, extended family, friends and schoolteachers. Ask your child to draw an outline of her outstretched hand and then to identify one person in her network to coincide with each finger. Later, when she is feeling down, she can refer to her drawing and decide whose help to seek.

Rachel, a young woman with two older sisters with intellectual disabilities, talked earlier in this book about her struggles with low self-esteem and subsequent depression. She had little social support. When asked what she would have liked as a child growing up, she said:

> **To know of other children my age who were 'normal' but had disabled sibs, to be able to meet them, write to them, talk with them, share with them, especially as we grew up and faced different challenges.**

To know that I wasn't as alone as I felt I was.

To be told often, in a language I could understand (meaning the explanations could get more complex as I got older), what was wrong with my siblings, and what my parents or the medical field seemed to think caused it.

To be told over and over again that it was okay that I was okay, even though my sisters are disabled and I am not, that it was not my fault, and that I should try to *not* feel guilty about the situation.

To have creative ways to express the guilt I would still feel.

To have some one-on-one time with my parents.

To not have to baby-sit my older siblings, and miss out on things that were important in my life because I was baby-sitting them.

To have had my interests more supported *without* my disabled siblings doing the same thing.

To have had the opportunity to get mad at my sisters and learn how to express it appropriately, so that it wouldn't be so difficult for me now as an adult to express anger.

To have had more than one telephone and more than one television in the house.

As I got older to have had clear written information: Who are my sisters' doctors? Who are the contact people for the places they live? Who is in charge of their work program?

Other factors that influence adjustment

Earlier I said that it is the characteristics of a family itself that most significantly influence a sibling's adjustment to living with a child with special needs. This chapter has explored ways in which parents can support siblings. I now want to look at a few other factors that have an influence: the nature of the disability, age factors, and the number of children in the family. Although these factors can be difficult or impossible to change, it might help if you understand their influence.

The nature of the disability

The type and severity of their brother's or sister's disability can influence siblings' reactions. Certain conditions may be difficult to explain to a sibling and might induce major behavioural problems in the child with a disability that disrupt family life. Family routines can be turned upside down and sleepless nights become the norm. In extreme cases siblings live in fear for their lives and the lives of other family members. Some disabilities mean a child is not able to respond to others, and a sibling might feel distressed after making unsuccessful attempts to engage the brother or sister in play or other activities. Where a child requires large amounts of care, some of this responsibility may be given to siblings. Some disabilities make siblings more embarrassed than others.

If the disability is not too severe, siblings may identify strongly with their brother or sister. They may therefore feel more discomfort, especially in shared social situations, because they might be afraid that people will think they, too, have a disability. A sibling spoke earlier about her embarrassment when her sister, who is deaf but looks 'normal', made strange sounds in public. When special treatment is given to a child whose disability isn't obvious, it might seem like favouritism to a sibling.

Age factors

The reactions of siblings may vary at different ages. It can be useful to consider the adjustment of siblings in terms of the following developmental stages:

Pre-school

Very young children are concerned about the attention they receive from parents. They may feel jealousy over the attention a sibling with special needs is given. Parents may be less available to an able child, both practically and emotionally, and this can affect a child's sense of security. Much has been written about the importance to a child of bonding with a parent, particularly during the first three years.

During these early years children will gradually move from independent play to a more shared experience. Because shared play can be problematic with a child with special needs, a younger sibling may be slower than her peers to develop communication and social skills. At the same time, even though there may be some frustration due to difficult interaction, young children will usually accept a child with special needs and adapt to any limitations that might manifest themselves.

Young children might have difficulty expressing the feelings they experience; they may have limited ability to label and identify the feelings. They might develop fears that they were to blame for the disability and that they might develop a disability themselves.

Most young siblings gain satisfaction from being 'mummy's little helper'. This can be an important factor in developing self-esteem and close relationships. It can, however, get out of balance if the child's own need for attention is not met.

Five to 12 years

As children move into the school years they can develop a greater understanding of what their sibling's special needs mean for both themselves and their brother or sister. They are also more aware of limitations that might restrict family activities, especially their own activities with peers.

Interactions with a brother or sister will continue to affect their social skill development. Siblings will become more conscious of peer reactions and might have difficulty explaining the special needs of a brother or sister to friends and other social contacts. They might feel embarrassment and avoid bringing friends home.

They might become more involved in a 'teacher role', which can add to their sense of competence and value. Difficulties arise if they cannot interact with a brother or sister in a normal sibling way, or if the responsibility becomes so burdensome that their own activities are restricted.

Teen years

Teenage siblings might have difficulty developing their own identity. This might be due to over-identification with the child with special needs or their own sense of guilt about developing independence.

There might be increased embarrassment and siblings might go through periods of not wanting to be seen with their brother or sister. But remember that most teenagers are sometimes embarrassed by their brother or sister.

They are likely to have greater understanding than their peers of the differences between people and, like all teenagers, will be trying to make sense of their own feelings and values, and the 'meaning of life'. They might begin to be concerned about the future of their brother or sister, and the role they will be expected or want to play. They will have concerns about finding a partner in life who will accept the possible responsibilities, and might consider their own risks of having a child with special needs.

Career choice might also be influenced by their family situation.

Adult years

The responsibility siblings feel for a brother or sister will usually become more focused as their parents grow older. Siblings may start to worry about their brother's or sister's future accommodation, financial issues and medical care. Some will become guardians. Some will have a brother or sister live with them. If a family has not discussed the future care of a person with special needs, the process for a sibling can become quite complicated.

Whatever the situation, the responsibility can be significant and affect not only the sibling's life choices, but also her relationships with others.

Birth order

Birth order is a factor too. An older child who has a younger brother or sister with a disability has lived for some time in a family without disability, has developed communication patterns with parents and, to some extent, developed his own identity and social networks. He is more likely than a younger sibling to understand the explanations given to him about his brother or sister, and the loss of parental attention. Older siblings may have more nurturing feelings towards a younger brother or sister with disabilities because they have known the child as a baby. On the other hand, they will have been present through the stress and possible uncertainty of diagnosis. They will experience greater disruption to normal family routines and may feel resentment about the changes. They may be expected to provide more care giving. Research has shown this to be particularly true for older sisters. Also, having anticipated a new playmate, an older child may be more aware of the losses involved.

Siblings who are younger than their brother or sister with a disability may be less likely to have been given clear explanations of the situation. They usually accept life as it is and may take several years to understand how their family differs from others. They may resent the attention given to a brother or sister with a disability but have less understanding in the early years of why it happens. If there are no other siblings, they might miss out on learning the usual give and take, exchange of emotions and various social skills that children often acquire in interaction with their brothers and sisters. As time goes on, they may be confused about having to act as the 'older' sibling and care for their brother or sister. Having greater abilities than an older brother or sister may heighten the 'survivor guilt'.

One mother talks of her two daughters' reactions. The daughter who is older than the child with a disability has grown up with her brother and accepts him well. The younger one wants him out of her life. The sibling's personality and experience will have an influence but birth order may also be a factor in their different attitudes. Each family system is complex, and parents might be at different stages of adjustment themselves when children are born.

When the ages of children are very close, it may be harder for a sibling to establish a separate identity because she identifies so closely with her brother or sister. This can be exacerbated in same-sex siblings and twins. One mother explains that her young daughter needed help from a psychologist to enable her to go through the 'normal' developmental stages that her older sister with disabilities could not. She identified so closely with her sister that she found it difficult to feel comfortable about her own abilities. Because of this close identification, siblings may feel a special empathy for their brother or sister and wonder what their experience is like.

Many of the same age factors may also come into play if the special needs arise later in a child's life.

One social worker who has worked with siblings says that older siblings often take on a parent role to younger siblings without special needs in order to free up parents to care for the child with special needs. Her impression is that younger siblings tend to develop more attention-seeking and problem behaviours. She adds that in her experience most siblings seem to struggle with fear, guilt, anger and grief. Further research could help us understand the influence of age factors.

The number of siblings in the family

The number of children in a family seems to be especially important. Siblings who are the only other child seem to have a more difficult time. They often yearn for another sibling with whom they can have a 'normal' relationship – a brother or sister who they can form allegiences with, and who will support them in their growth to independence. They may feel sad if the brother or sister is not able or willing to play in ways the sibling would like. Sometimes a sibling may feel more like a parent than a brother or sister. These children may miss some of the social skills development that usually occurs with siblings.

Single siblings and their parents often have difficulty identifying 'normal' sibling responses and blame all tensions in the relationship between the child with a disability and the able child on the disability instead of normal family sibling rivalry or the emotional chaos caused by puberty problems.

In some ways, a single sibling is like an only child. But because of the necessity for parents to devote large amounts of time to the child with special needs, the able child is unlikely to enjoy the same amount of individual interaction with parents that an only child enjoys. The child may have to participate in activities with just one parent while the other parent cares for the child with disabilities.

A single sibling may feel that all of her parents' hopes and dreams rest with her. She may constantly seek their approval. She may wish to make up to parents for a sister or brother's limitations and to protect the parents from more distress. This may eventually lead to a child ignoring her own needs, hiding her own illnesses or emotions, or other similar reactions.

A larger family throws even more complex interactions into the mix. Having a companion and confidante allows a child to share experiences, and so realise he or she is not the only one to have mixed feelings. It is easier to cope with those times when parents need to give more attention to the child with a disability. There may be less pressure (perceived or imposed) to succeed. There are more hands to help and more to share the load when siblings need to take over more responsibility as parents age.

Other brothers and sisters also act as a buffer to the stresses involved. Julie's older sister contracted encephalitis after a bout of measles when she was nine, and became brain damaged.

Julie was seven at the time, and had younger twin brothers. She remembers her reactions to her sister's illness and change in behaviour.

> **My sister and I had been very close and played together constantly. When she became sick, I missed her, but immediately switched my allegiance to my brothers. We played wonderful games. Missing my sister did not last too long because I had other siblings. It would have been *very* different if I didn't have them. It shows the enormous flexibility of children; I just swapped.**

On the other hand, not all siblings provide support to each other. Because of different experiences with or reactions to the child with a disability, able siblings may be driven apart. One might take on the role of 'caretaking sibling' while the other might get lumbered with the 'bad sibling' or 'uninvolved sibling' role, some of this by choice and some by parental pressure, birth order, gender and so on. Overall, though, it would seem that it is easier on siblings if there are other brothers or sisters.

When a child dies

The death of a child can create a range of confusing reactions for siblings – sadness, fear, anger and guilt. The role of siblings in the family will be changed forever. There will be a change in family order – the middle child may become the eldest, or a child may become an only child, with a huge sense of needing to make up to parents for the loss of the other child. Such children lose a shared history, a playmate and confidante. They may be fearful about the future and angry at parents, the brother or sister who died or professionals who cared for them. Siblings may feel guilty if they had negative thoughts about their brother or sister before their death. Of course, a sibling can experience these same changes when a sibling dies from any cause. Children mourn differently from adults. The processing of the grief may cover a range of developmental stages as they mature. The meanings they give to death will also change as they develop. Children may feel different and isolated from peers.

If a child has an illness, the time leading up to his or her death can sometimes be a time of closeness and family support.

There is less risk of longer-term emotional problems if the ill child's sibling is surrounded by loving support, is allowed to be involved in the care of the ill child, and is allowed to express his or her range of emotions. This period will sometimes involve extremely difficult decisions, such as whether to continue life support. If siblings are older it is best if they are involved in these discussions.

Sara Fleming, a paediatric palliative care nurse, confirms that no matter what the circumstances, all children who experience the death of a brother or sister need the same things.

> **In my experience, regardless of the details, the death of a child involves similar degrees of suffering and the notion of loss doesn't vary much. For siblings the journey through illness to death will carry its own specifics but there are some salient common experiences in bereavement and subsequent needs through mourning. They all need clear information, involvement in ritual and decisions, avenues for expression of feelings, reassurance and affirmation.**

In her book *The Grief of Our Children*, Dianne McKissock talks about a range of ways we can support children who are grieving the loss of a sibling. As in other situations discussed in this book, the most important thing we can give to children is the acknowledgement and understanding of their feelings. They need to know they can express their feelings without rejection.

Memories are a very important part of the grieving process. Sara tells the following story to highlight how children can be helped to deal with concerns about this.

> **Charlie was an 11-year-old sibling of a teenage girl, Lucy, who had a degenerative condition and a short lifespan prognosis. Following clinical indicators of a new phase in disease progress, Lucy was referred to the Palliative Care Service. At this time their parents gently told the siblings about the likelihood that Lucy would die sometime in the next few years. Charlie was very anxious, especially about the possibility of forgetting her sister. We talked about special memories and Charlie and her mother set off to find a special box. Charlie has since decorated her special chest and is collecting memory items of places they go, and writing in a journal that lives in the chest.**

It is important that in keeping memories, a family does not glorify the child who died. In this situation, siblings may feel they can never fill shoes of the dead brother or sister. Sometimes activities that seem foreign to adults can be a huge source of comfort to children. We need to be flexible to allow children to mourn in ways that feel right for them. Sara adds:

> **The sight of a child's grave in a big cemetery is often a source of distress. For many younger siblings the cool, hard starkness of the physical burial place is confronting to their memories of a vibrant child. Some families like to decorate these places so that the child shines through.**
>
> **Becky put fairy stickers on her sister's plaque in the wall, she has a fairy garden in memory of her sister at home. Melanie and Kim decorated their brother's headstone for Christmas.**

It is important for children to be allowed to do whatever makes it easier for them to cope with what is happening.

Support groups for bereaved siblings have been especially helpful in assisting siblings to cope with their feelings. They allow siblings to share their anger, fear and guilt in a place where others understand. They might be given the chance to express things they didn't get to say to the child who died. They can ask questions they may not have felt comfortable asking in other settings. In addition they can allow themselves to start to participate in fun activities again and feel okay about that. Some groups will include activities that help a sibling to collect and keep memories of their brother or sister who has died.

Summary

In order to grow into emotionally strong adults, siblings need:

- Clear information.
- To be included in discussions.
- Opportunities to share their feelings and experiences.
- To feel competent.
- To feel special.
- To be seen as a valued participant in supporting a brother or sister with special needs.

- A sense that they can influence what happens around them.
- Contact with other siblings.
- A strong network of social support.

12

The role of service providers

The term 'service providers' refers to a range of organisations and individuals with which a family might come in contact in its search for support. Organisations might include hospitals, disability services and schools. Individuals include doctors, nurses, physiotherapists, speech pathologists, psychologists and teachers, all of whom can play an enormous role in helping a family adjust.

How effective individual service providers can be in supporting families depends on their own professional training, personal interests and attitudes, as well as on the general philosophy of the organisation that employs them.

Some organisations support family-centred/whole-family approaches. Others tend to focus on the child with special needs and their main caregiver, while largely excluding the wider family. Some take a preventative approach, where they try to avoid problems developing. Others operate largely through crisis management, where they wait for problems to arise before taking action.

An organisation may see the benefits of adopting a preventative approach rather than one that is problem-focused, but government funding policies may restrict the services it is able to offer. Sadly, at this time, few services in Australia or overseas can access sufficient funds to develop family, and in particular, sibling services. The services that do operate rely on the personal commitment and professional advocacy of individuals.

This chapter tells parents what they can expect from the service system. I also hope that it will help service providers develop a context for the work they do and provide ideas to enhance what they already do.

Organisational policy and approach

For service providers to be able to support families effectively the agency that employs them needs to be committed to providing such support. In my experience, and that of other siblings, this requires the agency to adopt policies that encourage true family-centred care, provide support to *all* family members and focus on prevention.

Family-centred care

Family-centred care involves a shift from the traditional model of the professional as the sole expert. Service providers are gradually recognising that any working relationship between professionals and a family needs to be a true two-way process of give and take. Families often have much to contribute when decisions are being made about the care of their child. After all, the management of a disability or chronic illness involves the whole family and its day-to-day routines.

A young mother was upset with her treatment by a large organisation. A speech pathologist had come to a family meeting to discuss treatment options for the woman's young child. The speech pathologist had made it clear that 'this is what will be done'; she did not allow the mother any opportunities to make her own input. The mother felt like saying, 'Hey, I know my child, shouldn't you be asking what I think?' In addition, the organisation failed to provide this mother with a piece of equipment that would have given support to her child, who had walking difficulties. On both counts the mother was afraid to complain, feeling that her complaint might rebound negatively on her daughter. That may or may not have been true, but many parents in this situation feel vulnerable themselves and protective of their child with special needs. The speech pathologist needs to ask herself, 'Am I doing my best to try and help this family feel competent and feel they have some influence over what is happening to them?' Providers in general should make a point of asking families during an interview: 'Is there anything you don't understand? Is there anything more we can do to help you? Is there anything more you require of us?'

Families need help in accessing resources and developing skills that make them feel better able to help themselves. With service provider assistance, they can feel more confident about supporting each other within the family and seeking help from outside the family when necessary. Providers can help a family assess its own needs, determine the most likely places to gain support, and then become more competent in accessing that support. Again, not only is it important that a family has its needs met, but it is also important *how* the needs are met.

Whole-family approach

While family-centred care is a welcome change in direction that seems to be gaining popularity, the idea of broadening the approach to the whole family is still not pursued as widely as it ought to be.

Services have traditionally focused on the patient or client. Even when a family-centred perspective is taken, often the focus is on the parents and the child with the disability, without much attention given to siblings. Indeed, the focus is often on the mother/child pair – even fathers are left out.

Funding restrictions may contribute to the narrow focus of service delivery. But what happens to one family member clearly impacts on all the other members and it is unrealistic to consider the needs of one or two family members in isolation.

If we support the whole family, we are supporting the person with special needs. Surely children with special needs will progress much further when both parents and siblings are able to feel competent and emotionally supported, and the whole family can function in a positive, caring manner.

Sibling relationships are usually the longest of any intra-family relationships. Siblings play a crucial role in each other's development, and it seems short-sighted that they are often ignored by service providers. Siblings have much to contribute and much to gain by being involved.

Brothers and sisters are an important part of the social network, both for parents and the person with special needs. They also educate others. Their role changes as parents age. If siblings are supported, and have their feelings validated and needs met, they are much more likely to continue their relationship with their brother or sister, add to their quality of life, and be able to supplement available social services.

Prevention

In many societies there is a growing awareness of mental-health issues and the link between childhood experiences and adult mental health. People now understand that in order to reduce the likelihood of mental-health problems it is necessary to intervene early in a child's life, especially when a child experiences major difficulties.

From the stories told to me, it seems that siblings of people with special needs are at risk of developing emotional and mental health problems. It is clear that appropriate support from an early age increases the likelihood that a sibling will adjust more positively to her situation.

Sibling support is not merely an attempt to make siblings feel better, it is an important preventative mental-health strategy. Without intervention, the cost to a sibling and the cost to social services in later years can be high. On the other hand, with intervention, siblings are likely to have higher self-esteem and an enhanced sense of competence. They can also develop a range of positive human qualities, including compassion, tolerance and maturity.

There are various types of mental-health prevention. Some models target the whole population. Others target those populations that are identified as having a high risk of developing problems, while some target groups that already show signs of problems.

Many child mental-health services continue to focus on fixing problem behaviour. But many siblings do not show problem behaviour. Siblings may internalise their feelings and become the 'good child' or the 'super-helper', while at the same time struggling with feelings of isolation and self-abnegation. Many actually feel rewarded if they look after themselves and so hesitate to show their distress or seek help.

We need to identify populations of children who are at greater risk of developing problems later in life. Siblings of children with special needs are a high-risk group. There are, however, factors that protect such children from developing emotional or mental health problems – for instance clear information about their brother's or sister's special needs; a supportive, communicative family; the ability to feel competent; a strong social support network. Service providers need to make efforts to improve these protective factors for these children. Their aim should be to help children become more resilient. A resilient child is more able to recover from difficult situations, develop the capacity to overcome challenges and develop into a healthy, functioning adult. In fact, people who have experienced difficult times in childhood, had support and developed the skills to cope, often grow into much stronger adults.

The tools a sibling needs in order to become stronger and more resilient are ones that all children can use: the ability to identify and express their feelings, problem-solving skills, strategies to cope with daily frustrations and a sense of competence. They also need an adult who listens to and validates them. In order to improve the protective factors in a child's life, service providers must focus not only on the child himself but also the environments in which he operates – family, school and social.

The stresses on the whole family of a child with special needs can lead to a breakdown in family functioning and the ability of members of a family to support each other. If parents are given the right type of support early, we can prevent a family system losing balance. Developing communication skills and creating an environment that values each family member are important ways to improve support within a family.

Schools can be an important source of support and prevention. I explore this in more detail later in this chapter.

Finally, there needs to be more collaboration between child health workers, school personnel and community groups so that more effective systems of support can be developed for families and, in particular, siblings. Mentoring by a significant adult, peer support and social support can all be protective factors.

Service providers as advocates

Providers can play a major role in increasing the awareness of family (and sibling) issues among other professionals. They can encourage collaboration between different support agencies. They can ask friends, schools, extended family and the general community to improve the support available.

Professional training programs

Much of the training that health professionals receive is focused on crisis management and one-on-one interventions. Most

A checklist for agencies

The following checklist can be used as a starting point to assess whether an organisation's efforts to support families include principles of family-centred care, a whole-family approach and preventative measures. Does the agency/organisation:

Have policies that reflect a commitment to family-centred care, a whole-family approach and prevention?

Educate staff about the concerns of families and siblings when the family includes a child with special needs?

If appropriate, encourage research into what helps a family, and siblings in particular, to adjust positively?

Have mechanisms for ensuring effective collaboration between parents, older siblings and professionals?

Encourage parents and siblings to be involved in consultation groups, up to Board level? (This applies to larger organisations.)

Encourage parents whose children are newly diagnosed to have contact with parents who have already 'been there' and who know the system?

Provide programs specifically for siblings at different age levels?

Encourage siblings to be valuable members of the treatment team?

Have mechanisms in place to care for siblings in particularly stressful emergency situations? (This applies particularly to hospitals.)

Provide links with community services for families, such as respite, transport and peer support programs?

Encourage collaboration with different support agencies, and advocate for siblings to be included?

preventative efforts, on the other hand, focus on group or systemic (eg family) interventions.

A wide range of health professionals are in a prime position to influence how families adjust, and to support all members of a family, individually and collectively, to live with a child or family member with special needs. Parents may hesitate to see a counsellor but will often express their feelings to service providers who are involved with their child. These professionals, however, aren't always trained in interpersonal skills. Nor do they necessarily know the best ways to support a whole family. We need to ensure health professionals have some knowledge of how family systems work and have the necessary skills to provide support themselves, or know how to direct a family to appropriate services.

Professional training courses (eg medicine, nursing, social work, psychology, physiotherapy) should include: issues relating to whole family adjustment when there is a child with a disability or chronic illness; training in interpersonal skills; and training in how best to work collaboratively with families and other service providers.

In addition, I believe ongoing training and access to relevant information, especially in relation to sibling support, needs to become a priority for currently employed health professionals so they are better prepared to provide an appropriate and effective service.

Supporting parents

The first step in supporting siblings is to support parents. It is important to see a family as a system and recognise that *all* members of a family will be affected by what happens within that system. Different members of the family may react differently to what is happening. Service providers need to regard fathers and siblings as important members of the family system, both in need of support and capable of contributing support to others. Some fathers have said they feel actively excluded from various services. Providers should try to hold at least some meetings when both parents can attend. Both parents need to be addressed in interviews.

A family is also part of an overall social system. A family will influence and be influenced by other parts of the social system, including extended family, friends, work, school and the general community.

The following list describes the ways in which parents can be supported. A family-friendly provider will enable parents to:

Access information

Parents should be able to obtain information about their child's special needs and the resources that they can use in managing those needs. This information may need to be reinforced at a later

A checklist for professional training courses

Do opportunities exist for professionals to learn directly from parents and siblings about their support needs?

Are there training programs that raise awareness about the problems faced by families and siblings of a child with special needs?

Do parents and siblings participate in the development of training programs?

Do such programs include methods for working collaboratively with families?

Do they include training in interpersonal/counselling skills?

Do they include components that deal with family-centred practices and emerging theories of strengthening families?

Is there a focus on prevention as well as crisis management?

stage, when they are more ready, or it may need to be given again in a different way. It is important that service providers use language that is easily understood. The level of understanding within a family may need to be checked from time to time. Providers can ask parents to relay back what they have been told or asked to do. Merely asking 'Do you understand?' almost always elicits a 'Yes'.

At a gathering of parents I attended, all parents said there should be a package of information about services given to each family as soon as a diagnosis is made. Certainly some organisations do this, but not all.

Feel listened to

Part of feeling supported is feeling that others understand. Families can often be intimidated by professionals and feel they are seen as just another 'case'. Parents need to talk about their fears for the future, both for their child and the family. They need to show emotion. It can be easy for service providers to do a lot of talking, but there needs to be time for listening and for allowing a family to tell its story without guilt. If families are shown understanding they are better able to identify and ask for what they want and need. If service providers are open and honest, families will be encouraged to be the same. It is a matter of developing trust.

Providers need to be sensitive to cultural and language differences, as cultural attitudes might be relevant. These might include attitudes to disability, attitudes to caring roles within the family or attitudes to the use of support services. If the family has difficulty communicating in English, interpreting services should be used to elicit and convey information. This is preferable to using a bilingual family member or friend, who might under stress misinterpret what is being said.

Communicate openly with each other

Families can be shown skills to identify feelings and be open about them. They can be helped to give information to others in the family, for instance through regular family meetings. In some cases it might be helpful to refer a family for family therapy.

Regain a sense of competence

Shared responsibility can help families rebuild a sense of worth. Following diagnosis, parents in particular can feel totally lost. They may feel overwhelmed by grief and by the many decisions that need to be made. They can gradually regain their sense of control and self-confidence by having a role in decision-making. They also need skills in problem-solving and stress-management. Sometimes parents will respond more to programs with an educational focus rather than a support group. This needs to be kept in mind when planning programs.

Parents have unique knowledge of their child and their family. It is more effective to improve a family's capacity to help itself than to foster dependency on health professionals.

Like children, adults develop self-esteem through mastering situations and overcoming obstacles. Families need to know that *they* are steering the ship, with services to support them.

Sweeping statements such as 'You are *so* wonderful' put parents on a pedestal and add to the pressure – what if they *don't* always feel so wonderful? More specific statements – 'You really manage time well' or 'Your family seems to really care about each other' – can be taken on board more easily by most families. It is not helpful to say things like 'You were specially chosen for this task' or 'You must be very strong to be given this challenge.' Such messages can distance a family from a service provider. It is more helpful to acknowledge the difficulties for a family and then focus on how to work together to ensure the best outcome.

Families sometimes feel that others blame them for the problems they have. This can lead to low self-esteem and feelings of unworthiness. In the past and even now, to a lesser extent, some mothers have been blamed for their child's disability.

Sometimes it is necessary for service providers to ask a lot of questions. Parents who are feeling vulnerable and full of self-doubt and guilt may think the provider is trying to lay blame. The provider needs to explain why she is asking these questions. To strengthen a family we need to take the focus away from blame and concentrate on managing the situation.

Recognise the grief

Parents need help to identify and accept their feelings of loss and grief. This can sometimes be a complex process – each person's experience will be unique. Parents need help to accept that they are okay, no matter what their reaction. Service providers can help parents to see there is hope and their lives can be fulfilling in areas they may never have imagined. Providers should be careful, however, not to belittle the parents' difficulties and grief.

Parents need help to understand the nature of chronic sorrow. They are likely to experience recurring sorrow during different periods and parents can learn to prepare for these times. They will undergo a range of reactions and for some the process of adjustment will take months and years. Some parents, in the early stages, do not need to talk about their situation but instead need comfort from those around them, 'a blanket around the shoulder'.

Find new meaning

How parents perceive a disability or chronic illness will have a major impact on their adjustment. The messages that society and their social network give them will influence this to a large extent. In some families each member will eventually be able to take pride in each other, gain self-confidence and have a clear sense of purpose. Other families will have difficulty moving toward such a positive position. Providers need to be wary of trying to put their own meaning on the situation but they can have a big influence on how parents see things. Parents can be helped to focus on the immediate steps.

Practitioners need to help parents understand their own feelings and how these influence not only their own behaviour and attitudes but the reactions of those around them. Are their thoughts helpful? Are their thoughts telling them the situation will *never* get better? Are they putting a lot of blame on themselves?

Parents may go through a period of denial following diagnosis. As long as it doesn't continue so long that it puts the child with special needs or siblings at risk, this can be a healthy coping mechanism. Service providers may be tempted to confront this denial, but that may be counter-productive. Of course, if the denial becomes entrenched it can be difficult for siblings in particular to make sense of what is happening because they are told one thing but observe another.

Access appropriate services and resources

Providers can play a crucial role in enabling families to access services that are suitable for them and provide both practical and emotional support. Respite is crucial for parents and siblings. All relevant service providers need to advocate for more services to be made available especially just after diagnosis.

Have contact with other families

Providers should encourage parents to have contact with other parents of children with disabilities.

Many groups exist in Australia where parents get together for discussion or social activities. These groups can give both practical and emotional support. They help parents develop their own coping skills and help them develop a more positive view of themselves and their child with a disability. Some parents may need time before they are ready to belong to a support group but they need to know such groups exist. Some organisations bring together whole families to share support.

Strengthen and improve the network of social support

Sometimes parents need help in explaining the special needs to family and friends and in enlisting their support.

Service providers might also encourage parents to create wider networks. Both providers and the community need to be creative and committed in developing new preventative, supportive approaches. For example, programs could be developed where trained volunteers are assigned to a family with the aim of providing a listening ear as well as practical help.

Why siblings don't access services

The need for specific sibling support is still largely unrecognised in the community and siblings rarely access services, either those provided through disability organisations or more general services. Some reasons for this might include:

Sibling guilt

Siblings are often given – and believe – messages that they should feel lucky. What are their problems compared to their brother's or sister's? They don't want to add to the considerable burden parents may face, so they try to be the 'good' child. This may make them reticent to express their own pain or confusion, and reluctant to seek support.

Problems not recognised within family

Parents may be too preoccupied with the child with special needs to recognise the sibling is having problems. In some cases, parents are struggling with their own stress, grief and acceptance and their emotional resources are stretched to the absolute limit. They don't always identify the signs of distress in their children and, therefore, don't see the need for support.

Problems not recognised by service providers

Health professionals, teachers and other providers often lack understanding of the issues for siblings. This can hinder their ability to respond to a sibling in a supportive way. It is relatively easy for mental health professionals to understand the deleterious effects on a child whose parents are dealing with alcoholism or mental illness, or who physically or emotionally abuse their children. With siblings of children with special needs the issues can be more complex and much less clear. Even in families that seem to be adjusting well, siblings can develop problems if not supported. Health professionals who do understand sibling issues are often restricted in what they can do, due to limited funding.

Supporting siblings

Families should be able to count on services to provide support to siblings. Service providers can support parents and thereby give them the strength to support their children, or providers can intervene directly with siblings. Sibling support requires knowledge of disability and family issues. If a provider has the opportunity, and if he has child-counselling skills, he can give the sibling individual counselling. Siblings can also be supported through groups. Siblings may need different support at different times in their lives.

Helping children become more resilient involves giving them skills that enable them to cope with stresses. In this regard even minimal interventions can make a marked difference. For example, many adult siblings suggest their own adjustment as children would have been better had they been introduced to other siblings who struggled with similar issues. My own experience in working with families supports this.

In order to support siblings, service providers should aim to:

Give information

Siblings need information about how the special needs affect their brother or sister and the rest of the family. For example, if their brother or sister is in hospital, siblings need information about who is looking after the child, what is happening and how long the child is likely to be hospitalised. Without information, a sibling's fears will grow. Siblings also need to know they are not to blame for their brother's or sister's disability or illness. Nor are they to blame for the family's difficulties or the distress of their parents. Siblings should be included in most of the discussions about the child with special needs.

Show an interest in siblings

Providers can ask siblings about school, their friends, and their hobbies. If children express concerns, or show difficulty in adjusting – for instance if they claim not to have friends or hobbies – they can be offered support. By building relationships with siblings, service providers can help them feel important and special.

Encourage siblings to talk about their feelings

Siblings need to discuss both the good and not-so-good feelings. Comments like, 'If I had a brother with X, I think sometimes I might feel a bit angry. How about you?' give children permission to express their feelings. With the consent of the parents, you could offer them someone (either yourself or another appropriate professional) to talk to in confidence. Siblings can learn that their concerns are normal.

Some siblings will show signs of distress through their behaviour, but others hide their true feelings. It can be helpful to discuss the idea that we all have strengths and weaknesses, including the child with a disability. A sibling needs to know how he is similar to and different from his brother or sister with special needs.

Acknowledge the care a sibling gives to the child with special needs

A provider can ask a sibling's opinion and help her discover opportunities to contribute in positive ways. Being involved in decisions and being given small responsibilities in relation to the child with special needs will help the sibling feel valued and competent.

Sweeping statements can make siblings feel inadequate and guilty. A comment like, 'Aren't you a wonderful sister!' will only make the sibling feel worse if she doesn't in fact feel she is coping well. It is more helpful to make concrete statements such as: 'When you do that for your brother it really helps him learn to talk.'

Give siblings skills to deal with stressful situations

These skills might include constructive ways of dealing with emotions. Service providers can teach children problem-solving skills to cope with a variety of situations. There is a range of models that can be used. One, the STOP, THINK, DO model, is part of an overall program of teaching social skills and managing behaviour in both primary and secondary school students.

Developed by clinical psychologists (Petersen and Gannoni, in their book *Teachers' Manual for Training Social Skills while Managing Student Behaviour*), this method uses a traffic light symbol to remind children of the process. All children can use the method when faced with problems that seem insurmountable. STOP (red) reminds children (and adults, including teachers and parents) to stop before they rush into anything and act impulsively. They then clarify the problem and how they and others might be feeling and what they want to happen next. THINK (yellow) reminds children to think about and generate many possible alternative solutions to the problem. Solutions may include fighting, telling an adult, demanding, asking nicely, bargaining, sharing/compromising or walking away. Depending on the problem, other solutions can be discussed too. Children also think of the consequences of each solution and how people feel about them. DO (green) reminds children to choose the best solution (the one with the most acceptable consequences) and put it into action. If it doesn't work, they can go back to STOP and evaluate what went wrong. Maybe the problem was different to what they thought, or the strategies inappropriate, or their behaviour was not as they had planned. After they have done that they can THINK of something else to DO.

Sibling groups are an ideal venue to think about possible solutions and consequences, but providers can work with individual siblings in order to develop problem-solving skills. Some of the different problems might include conflicts with peers such as teasing, with parents such as perceived favouritism, and with the child with special needs, for example disruptive behaviour. Such skills empower siblings and let them know that they can influence what happens to them. Providers can help siblings understand the link between their thoughts and their feelings, and develop more positive ways of looking at the world (this is covered further in chapter 11).

Help siblings develop independence

Families may need help to recognise a sibling's need to develop independence. Siblings can be helped to develop their own identity by looking at their interests and goals for the future.

Encourage attendance at a sibling group

Service providers can refer siblings to groups in their area or, if none exist, you could start one. (Resources available to help are listed at the end of this book.)

The main aims of a sibling group are to provide children with the opportunity to share feelings in a fun, safe environment, to increase their social networks and to develop strategies for dealing with problems. Some groups focus on enjoyable activities and certainly these can provide links with other siblings and opportunities to share experiences and feelings. It can be a missed opportunity, however, if the group or agency does not recognise the need for further intervention in skill development and enhancing competence. Many siblings feel powerless and learning skills to deal with difficult situations gives a sibling more of a sense of control.

Help the sibling identify formal support mechanisms

These 'mechanisms' might include service providers involved in the care of their brother or sister, or particular counsellors.

Assess how a sibling is doing socially

Help a sibling identify and develop her social networks. Peer relationships, social activities, school performance and family interactions are all indicators of how a sibling is managing. Having healthy social networks also helps siblings develop their independence.

Help siblings find the positives

While this is truly useful, it can be unhelpful to deny the reality of their situation. For some children the stresses are considerable and they will find it demoralising if you gloss over their experience. Adults often say to siblings, 'Oh, don't worry about it!' or 'Things aren't that bad.' It is far better to acknowledge the difficulty and then look for solutions. For example, saying to a sibling, 'Hey, I can understand you worrying about that,' shows the sibling you are listening and acknowledging their experience. It is then possible to move on and explore ways of making the situation less worrying.

Provide individual counselling

The aims of individual counselling are to help siblings understand, accept and express their reactions to having a brother or sister with a disability, to feel listened to, to learn ways of dealing with problems, and to develop self-esteem. Some siblings need help in finding their own identity and working out their goals for the future. The relationship with their brother or sister with special needs will often improve if their own needs are met in this way.

Part of the process, like all therapeutic interventions, involves the development of trust between the counsellor and child. Some children will need more in-depth counselling if they are going through particular difficulties and will need contact with a qualified child therapist.

Collaborate with other organisations

Many other organisations will have an influence on children's lives, for example schools, child health organisations and community groups.

School-based approaches

School can provide a further avenue for informal and formal social support of siblings. Programs for siblings run within schools, or even general disability awareness programs, can help give siblings the coping skills to deal with their situation. But every little extra attention can make a big difference. The support can be provided in a very informal way by improving the chance for siblings to develop social networks.

Unfortunately, sibling support in schools is still rare in Australia. In my experience there is little awareness about sibling issues among education agencies, many teachers and school counsellors. In addition, teachers and counsellors are often unaware of the fact when a child has a brother or sister with special needs. Many siblings internalise their difficulties. And when a sibling does display behavioural problems, authorities rarely recognise the cause.

In these days of reduced staff numbers many school psychologists can only take on a largely diagnostic role, rather than a preventative, therapeutic approach. School counsellors are in many schools, but there could be more, especially in primary schools, where preventative approaches could be most effective.

When I was a child, there must have been other students at my school who had a brother or sister with a disability. I didn't know of them and they didn't know of me. There was no one I could talk to about my sleepless nights, my embarrassment and loneliness. If only we had known each other through those times, known there were others dealing with similar issues and uncertainties, it would have balanced the negative messages we had from other sources. Such support would be very simple to provide.

A note to teachers

For many siblings, school itself is a welcome respite from the stresses of home but siblings can also bring the difficulties of their home life into school life. Siblings may be rebellious or they may have picked up inappropriate behaviour from a brother or sister with disabilities. They may have problems socially, perhaps because they have not learnt from their brother or sister the accepted ways of relating to those of a similar age. Siblings may display anxiety or they may internalise their emotions and show signs of depression. As one mother said about her daughter, 'She's a mess at school the days her sister is in hospital.' Some siblings will not wish to talk about a sibling with a disability;

others will feel comfortable doing so when young, but less so as they grow older.

If the child is comfortable (this is very important and needs to be established first) she could make a presentation to the class about her brother or sister with special needs. This could be part of a broader activity in which the class discusses different disabilities and in which it is acknowledged that individuals have different strengths and weaknesses. A parent of the sibling might also like to be involved. There might be more than one sibling in the class. (I mentioned earlier that this could possibly be engineered by the school.) Other children in the class might be cousins or friends of someone with special needs and they could also add to the discussion. Some disability agencies are able to provide such sessions as part of their outreach service.

It is best if activities that promote disability awareness and open communication can start at an early age.

For Nance, a particular teacher helped her find the positives in her situation.

> **I was lucky in my senior year of high school. I was taken under the wing to a degree by an English teacher, who I look back on now as one of the pivotal people in my life. Who knows where I would be now without her? She understood my rebellions, overlooked the silly ones, and gave me the opportunity to write about my brother in my school essays and express the frustration I felt. I know now, looking back, she basically helped me to grow up. Largely because of her I came to realise that just like any person, there were good points to my brother and bad. He was not necessarily a burden or someone to feel embarrassed about. He had his own special talents, such as memorising it seems almost every song ever written, that I could be proud of and share with him. And it was from then on, about 17 I suppose, that I became closer to him again and saw him primarily as a friend, rather than feeling bitter about what could have been.**

Teachers can also help siblings develop a sense of mastery, not only through academic skills but also sport, music, positions of responsibility and social skills. They can talk to students about using skills to solve problems through the normal course of a day.

Having a student in your class who is a sibling of someone with special needs provides an opportunity to incorporate a range of topics into the classroom. Issues around disability, accepting differences, showing empathy and building resilience can all be covered as part of disability awareness, health, society and environment studies.

Teachers can give direct support to siblings in the following ways.

- Encourage discussion about a brother or sister with special needs. Let siblings know you are available to talk.
- Be aware that in some cases it will be difficult for a sibling to complete homework; some may have problems with tiredness.
- If a sibling struggles with schoolwork try to find other activities that give them a sense of competence, such as art or music.
- Encourage siblings to write about their brother or sister in daily journals or story writing time. They can share their writing with you, keep it to themselves or tear it up. Even if they throw away their writing, the exercise itself can be very helpful.
- Put the child in touch with relevant resources, such as Siblings Australia, books and internet sites.
- Help the child to develop support networks with adults and same-age peers. These networks help a child feel valued and can encourage independence.
- Try to have the child get together with other siblings, either through the school or by referring him to other organisations.

Summary

It is important that providers, when trying to support families:

- Identify the needs of *all* members of a family.
- Focus on strengths without belittling the difficulties.
- Help family members recognise and acknowledge all the feelings they are experiencing.
- Enable a family to feel competent in being able to make choices and access support from within and outside the family.
- Put families in contact with others who have developed acceptance and coping skills.
- Enable families to identify and improve social networks.

Service providers can support siblings by:

- Helping them access information and involving them with their brother or sister.

- Allowing them to express the good and not-so-good feelings.
- Helping them realise that they too are special and valued.
- Helping them feel a sense of competence.
- Encouraging them to develop a wide support network, including professional support from service providers, teachers, general practitioners, counsellors; peer support for other siblings; and support from parents, their own siblings, friends and extended family.

This support ideally comes early, so problems are prevented. Siblings should be included in the support loop for families from the very beginning.

A final word

My introduction to *Siblings* included the words: 'I hope the ideas in this book will help build links between siblings, between parents and siblings and, finally, between practitioners and families.' Those links will only be forged, however, if families and practitioners are prepared to raise awareness of sibling needs and advocate for support.

If you are an adult sibling, try to talk to other siblings about your experiences, both the good and not so good ones. Become more involved in the organisation that supports your brother or sister. Investigate the possibility of becoming involved in a sibling program, either with other adult siblings or children. Email me with your story. Let me know your response to this book. You could join the discussion group for adult siblings on Siblings Australia website.

If you are a parent, check whether the disability organisation that supports you provides a sibling program or can direct you to one. If not, tell them about the growing network of parents, providers and siblings who are working to develop more support services. I have listed some organisations in the resources section of this book. There is a much more comprehensive list in the directory on Siblings Australia website, which will be updated regularly. If there is a program nearby, you could ask if it needs extra help. If there are no programs near you, contact Siblings Australia for information about starting a program. The Project can put you in touch with organisations across Australia, in which parents are the driving force behind sibling programs. Encourage your child to join a discussion group via the Siblings Australia website. There is one for teens and one for younger children, and both are moderated by the project.

As a practitioner, spread the word about sibling issues among your colleagues. Through the Siblings Australia website you can join a national discussion group for providers working in the area of sibling support. Encourage collaboration between different agencies that have a focus on preventative mental health, disability or education. Share your work with others. It is important that we all work to keep family and sibling support on the agenda.

Acknowledgements

Siblings is the result of a long journey over several years. A number of friends, relatives and colleagues gave personal support and encouragement along the way. Others gave ideas and feedback on the book itself. I am indebted to them all.

During a visit to the United States in 1998, Tom Keating of the Eugene Research Institute was extremely generous with his time, gave me access to a wide range of literature and helped me believe this book was possible. Don Meyer, Director of the Sibling Support Project, put me in touch with many adult siblings, enabling me to learn I was not alone.

At home, Dr David Rampling helped me enormously along my path of understanding and self-acceptance.

Paul Heinrich helped give structure to the book. David Cole helped me get started on the most important phase of my own personal journey. He also read early drafts and gave numerous helpful suggestions. Steve Maloney edited various drafts, and helped me gain 'permission' to proceed. Lesley Oliver and Valerie Aloa have always listened, given encouragement and been there for me.

Work colleagues, from both the mental health and disability sectors, helped me to formulate my ideas. In particular, Dr Jon Jureidini showed me that I could combine my personal and professional self. He was instrumental in both of my dreams, Siblings Australia and this book, becoming a reality. Jane Fitzgerald commented on sections of the book and helped put the theory into practice. Major input also came from Jayne Lehmann, Chris Egan, Tania Withington, Jane Tracy and Lesley McBain.

Numerous siblings and parents shared their hearts and thoughts with me. I hope you gained as much as I have in the process of opening up to others. You have all contributed to the increased awareness of the need to support siblings.

Editor Bronwen Gwynn-Jones and I shared frustration and pleasure as we gave shape to the evolving manuscript. Wakefield Press staff, especially Michael Bollen and Sheree Tirrell, gave the book its final form and I thank them for their faith.

My parents read through various versions of the manuscript, shared thoughts and, though it must have been difficult, continued to encourage me. They have given many gifts and shown me the true meaning of love and loyalty.

Special appreciation goes to my husband, Rob. From a less than enthusiastic response when I first raised the idea at 3 am, he went on to support this child of mine through the long gestation. He read and edited, and edited again, numerous versions of the manuscript. He, more than anyone, knows what an incredible ride this has been.

And finally, to my two daughters, Erin and Tess, who endured me writing at the computer incessantly and who went through their own periods of neglect – all I can say is 'Mum's back!' As daughters and as sisters, they are the most beautiful gift to me and to each other.

Resources

There are a number of Siblings projects around the world providing resources for families and practitioners. Kate Strohm manages Siblings Australia Inc. The website is updated regularly. www.siblingsaustralia.org.au email: info@siblingsaustralia.org.au

Sibling Project
Department of Psychological Medicine
Women's and Children's Hospital
72 King William Road
North Adelaide
South Australia 5006

Ph: (08) 8161 6737
Fax: (08) 8161 7032

Email: sibproject@wch.sa.gov.au
Website: www.wch.sa.gov.au/sibling

Books

Beckman, P. (ed.). (1996). *Strategies for Working with Families of Young Children with Disabilities*. Baltimore: Paul. H. Brookes.

Bluebond-Langner, M. (1996). *In the Shadow of Illness: Parents and siblings of the chronically ill child*. Princeton: Princeton University Press.

Borchere, D. *Fragile Secret*. See www.fragilesecret.com.

Bruce, E.J. & Schulz, C.L. (2001). *Nonfinite Loss and Grief: A psychoeducational approach*. Baltimore: Paul H. Brookes Publishing Co.

Cook, P. (1999). *Supporting Sick Children and Their Families*. London: Bailliere Tindall.

Featherstone, H. (1980). *A Difference in the Family: Living with a disabled child*. New York: Basic Books.

Fullwood, D. & Cronin, P. (1986). *Facing the Crowd: Managing other people's insensitivities to your disabled child*. Melbourne: Royal Victorian Institute for the Blind School.

Griffiths, K. (1997). *P.S. This Accident Has Changed Everyone and Everything: A guide to understanding head injury*. Melbourne: Shannon Books.

Harris, S.L. (1994). *Siblings of Children with Autism: A guide for families*. Bethesda, MD: Woodbine.

Harris, S.L. *et al.* (1994). *Siblings of Children with Autism: A guide for families* (2nd edn). Bethesda, MD: Woodbine House.

Hornby, G. (1994). *Counselling in Child Disability: Skills for working with parents*. London: Chapman & Hall.

Karasik, J. & Karasik, P. (2003). *The Ride Together: A brother and sister's memoir of autism in the family.* New York: Washington Square Press.

Klein, S.D. & Schleifer, M.J. (eds). (1993). *It Isn't Fair! Siblings of children with disabilities*. Westport, CT: Bergin & Garvey.

Kubler-Ross, E. (1969). *On Death and Dying*. New York: Macmillan.

Lobato, D.J. (1990). *Brothers, Sisters, and Special Needs: Information and activities for helping young siblings of children with chronic illnesses and developmental disabilities*. Baltimore: Paul H. Brookes.

McHugh, M. (1999a). *Special Siblings*. New York: Hyperion Press.

McHugh, M. (1999b). *Special Siblings Growing up with someone with a disability*. Baltimore, MD: Paul H. Brookes.

McKissock, D. (1998). *The Grief of Our Children*. Sydney: ABC Books.

Meyer, D. (ed.) (1997). *Views from Our Shoes: Growing up with a brother or sister with special needs*. Bethesda, MD: Woodbine.

Meyer, D.J. & Vadasy, P.F. (1994). *Sibshops: Workshops for brothers and sisters of children with special needs*. Baltimore: Paul H. Brookes.

Meyer, D.J. & Vadasy, P.F. (1996). *Living with a Brother or Sister with Special Needs: A book for sibs* (2nd edn). Seattle: University of Washington Press.

Orphan, A. (2004). *Moving On: Supporting parents of children with SEN.* London: David Fulton Publishers.

Petersen, L. & Gannoni, A.F. (1992). *Teachers' Manual for Training Social Skills while Managing Student Behaviour*. Victoria: The Australian Council for Educational Research.

Powell, T.H. & Gallagher, P.A. (1993). *Brothers and Sisters: A special part of exceptional families* (2nd edn). Baltimore: Paul H. Brookes.

Richey, D.D. & Wheeler, J.J. (2000). *Inclusive Early Childhood Education.* New York: Delmar Thomson Learning.

Seligman, M. & Darling, R. (1997). *Ordinary Families, Special Children: A systems approach to childhood disability.* New York: The Guilford Press.

Siegel, B. & Silverstein, S. (1994). *What About Me? Growing up with a developmentally disabled sibling.* New York: Plenum Press.

Simon, R. (2003). *Riding the Bus with My Sister: A true life journey.* New York: Plume Books.

Singer, G.H.S. & Powers, L.E. (1993). *Families, Disability and Empowerment: Active coping skills and strategies for family interventions.* Baltimore: Paul H. Brookes.

Fiction for young siblings

Byars, Betsy (1996). *The Summer of the Swans.* Demco Media.

Pulver, Robin and Wolf, Elizabeth (1999). *Way to Go, Alex!* Albert Whitman & Company.

Thompson, Mary (1992). *My Brother, Matthew.* Woodbine House.

UK sites

www.sibs.org.uk

Sibs is an organisation for brothers and sisters of people with special needs. info@sibs.org.uk; 01904 550029.

www.siblinks.org

SIBLINK is a website for young people with a brother or sister who has/had cancer.

www.sibspace.org

Tuberous Sclerosis Association siblings' website.

www.cafamily.org.uk

Contact a Family provides information on different conditions and links to specific condition groups. Parent and family helpline: 0808 808 3555.

www.kidscape.org.uk

Kidscape offers support and advice on dealing with bullying and teasing. 020 7730 3300.

www.winstonswish.org.uk

Winston's Wish supports bereaved children and young people. Family line 0845 203 0405.

www.crusebereavementcare.org.uk

Cruse Bereavement Care supports anyone who has been bereaved. 0870 167 1677.

www.carersonline.org.uk

Carers UK provides information, advice and support for carers. 020 7490 8818.

www.gig.org.uk

Genetic Interest Group supports people affected by genetic disorders/ diseases. 020 7704 3141.

Australian sites

www.carenet.org.au

Carenet, based in Melbourne, provides family-centred assistance to families who have a chronically/seriously ill child. There is a particular focus on siblings.

www.dmdforum.org

This site provides support and resources to the Duchenne Muscular Dystrophy Community. It includes a specific section on sibling issues.

www.sane.org

SANE Australia produces a range of easy-to-read publications and multimedia resources on mental illness and related topics, including *The SANE Guide for Brothers and Sisters: A guide for siblings of people living with mental illness.*

www.preemie-l.org/siblings.htm

This site looks at ways to support siblings of premature babies, with a range of ideas for parents and staff of neonatal intensive care units.

home.vicnet.net.au/~nnaami/resources.htm

A list of resources for families and siblings of people with mental illness.

United States sites

www.thearc.org/siblingsupport

The Sibling Support Project is a national program dedicated to the interests of brothers and sisters of people with special health and developmental needs. It hosts internet discussion groups for siblings and service providers, and offers the Sibshop training program.

www.familyvillage.wisc.edu/general/frc_sibl.htm

Family Village is a global community that integrates information, resources and communication opportunities on the internet for persons with cognitive and other disabilities, for their families, and for service providers.

www.faculty.fairfield.edu/fleitas/teasetips.html

This site gives a range of strategies for dealing with teasing, especially in relation to a brother or sister with disabilities.

Index